Financial Markets in a Nutshell

A Foundation for Understanding the Financial World

Christopher Radcliffe

ISBN: 978-1-7376329-0-0
eISBN: 978-1-7376329-1-7

This publication has been registered with the Library of Congress.

For my Grandparents

For my Parents

For my Siblings

For my Uncles and Aunts

For my Cousins

For Family

Love you all

TABLE OF CONTENTS

1.

Markets: What, Who, Where, When, Why

Have you ever overheard someone excitedly say something along the lines of "The Dow Jones was up 15 points today" or "My cryptocurrency investments finally paid off and I'm rich!"? Perhaps you have heard the opposite, and someone depressingly said, "I bought high and I sold low" or "I thought my portfolio was perfect, and now I have nothing!" Upon hearing this, perhaps you will give them an excited thumbs up and a "that's great buddy", or a pat on the back and tell them your "sorry to hear that." We then move on confused, not understanding what just came out of that person's mouth, and we leave to do something we actually enjoy. Until we are again confronted with terms like valuation, margin, IPO, and par value. All of these phrases seem to make sense to the people discussing them, but these phrases can be confusing and repetitive. This book will serve as a guide for the various financial markets and how they work. This book will not tell you whether or not your investment portfolio will rise or fall in value, but it may help you understand how to determine value in each specific market and how that value is traded.

When you first think of a financial market, the first thought that comes to mind may be of an extremely busy Wall Street floor where traders scream prices at each other as papers lay on the ground waiting to be retrieved. In reality, this image is extremely out of date as almost all trades take place using computers, and face to face transactions are almost unheard of. While the markets may have changed, the fundamental aspects of the markets have not. As a result, understanding these basic fundamentals will help us to make informed decisions and allow us to understand what people are saying when they talk about the various markets.

As a side note, I have organized this book to cover one financial market each chapter. If you are interested in a specific market but don't care for another, feel free to skip through chapters. Here are the Table of Contents again as nobody seems to ever read through them the first time.

What Markets Do?

Markets are diverse and each one is unique with its own qualities, but they all tend to accomplish the same goals. Here are some of the primary functions and results of financial markets.

Asset Valuation: The financial markets provide a way for specific assets to receive a set price. That price is whatever someone is willing to pay for it, no more and no less. With this, the markets help to determine exactly what an asset is worth. Think about it like this, you may be willing to pay $5 for a dozen eggs. If eggs are being sold for $10, you will not buy them because it is not worth the price. If the price instead is set to $4, then you will buy the eggs because they are worth it at that price. In a similar sense the financial markets are the same way, but the difference is that there are hundreds of millions of people that all have different ideas of what a dozen eggs should cost. This mental concept of what a dozen eggs should cost is completely subject to change. What millions of people are willing to pay for a dozen eggs changes based upon all available information. If a report is published that eggs can cause high cholesterol and are bad for your overall health, the price people are willing to pay for it may change. As a result, the price of eggs may have to be lowered to $2 so that people will buy it again. It should be noted that the opposite effect can be observed. Say a discovery is made that eggs are the source of long life and can extend life expectancy by 5 years. Then the price of eggs may increase as people try to eat their way to health. This is a silly illustration, but hopefully this example demonstrates how prices can change and fluctuate in the financial markets.

Raising Capital: Another function of the financial markets is their ability to raise capital for different companies. While this is not true of all the financial markets, it is especially important for the equity and debt markets. For example, a firm may need capital in order to finance a project or facility that will bring in more revenue for the firm. As a result, the company may issue equity (stocks) or debt (bonds) in order to finance their actions. More on the equity and debt markets in Chapter 2 and Chapter 3.

Investing: The main reason many investors enter the financial markets is to increase their wealth. The Equity, Debt, and Money Markets provide a way for individual investors to place funds that are not immediately needed to purchase assets. This way investors can receive a return on their investments and eventually turn those assets into a future income source.

Risk Management: Financial markets like the Foreign Exchange, Futures, and Options Markets provide an avenue to mitigate several types of risk. Typically, these are used by firms or individuals that do not know what the future value of what they are buying or selling will be. As a result, these types of exchanges can be used to help better determine what the future inflow or outflow of capital will be. These markets also allow a price to be attached to a lower risk exposure. Meaning that entities can choose to pay for a lower risk exposure in one area while deciding to not hedge their risk exposure in another area.

Who are in the Markets?

The people that are in the market will be classified into two groups. The first are individual investors. Individual investors are made up of several groups that act differently. The second type of investors are the institutional investors. Institutional investors are typically large pools of money or large banks that work directly on Wall

Street. To simplify this, I will be describing both of these investors in the simplest way possible.

Individual Investors

Long-Term Investors

These types of investors are in the market for the long-haul. They pretty much only do two actions throughout their lifetime. First, they buy, and then they hold until they die or pass it on to their children. Typically, this investor says "Buy the dip" and "Time in the market beats timing the market." When they get older, they will often retire and live off of the income that their investments generate every year.

Short-Term Traders

Also referred to as day traders, they typically exclusively trade on the stock market and will focus on trends that are quickly moving upwards or downwards. These traders will likely hold a stock for a few days and not hold a stock for more than a month before they jump onto the next stock that is "moving."

Speculators

These are short-term traders that have started trading options or futures. Speculators like to put large amounts if not all of their portfolio into a single position and see what happens. Some of the more advanced speculators love options where they either lose all the money that they put in or make massive amounts of money on a single trade.

Inflation Avoiders

These types of investors typically will throw their money into a money market account. Their money will pretty much just keep up with inflation and do absolutely nothing else. People do this when they are preparing to make a large purchase in less than a year and want to ensure that inflation doesn't lower the value of their funds.

Silver/Gold Investors

Also referred to as gold bugs, these investors will pay for a rock that was dug up in an African country. Bring that rock to their country of choice, and then put it right back into the ground or a bunker. Effectively, these investors buy an asset that provides zero income and goes up in value only when people are scared of an economic or societal collapse.

Institutional Investors

Institutional investors are companies that invest money on the behalf of individual investors. These investors will typically purchase large amounts of stocks and bonds at a time. As a result, they are often referred to as "whales."

Commercial Banks

The first "whale" are commercial banks. Commercial banks offer banking, lending, and investment services to individuals. Commercial banks take the general public's money to safeguard it, and then turn around and use that money to write loans to small businesses and other individuals. Effectively, they act as the financial intermediary between people with excess funds and people in need of funds. They perform an essential role in the overall economy by helping make the flow of capital easier and much more secure. Without financial intermediaries, people in need of funds would find it very difficult to obtain funding as people would not want to make loans because of the risky nature of receiving payment. A financial intermediary is able to hedge that risk by issuing thousands of loans and then knowing that some of those loans will likely go unpaid.

Endowment Funds

Endowment funds are a special type of investor. An endowment fund is set up by a foundation of some kind. Some foundations include universities, religious institutions, and other non-profits. For example, many private and public universities establish endowment funds. Contributions are made to the fund in the form of a donation. An example of this is when a college sends letters out to all their alumni asking them to "give back." You can rest assured that the money will likely be placed directly into an endowment fund. For a fun exercise go ahead and check the size of the endowment fund of the college you graduated from or are currently attending. I promise that you will be extremely surprised by the size of some of these funds. Typically, the more prestigious the institution the larger the fund. Check out Harvard and Yale's endowment funds if you want to be blown away.

Mutual Funds

Mutual funds are a well-known type of institutional investor. A mutual fund is an open investment fund for individual investors. Almost anybody is able to gain access to these types of funds. Mutual funds will then pool together money from all of the individual investors and invest that money. The money is managed by a portfolio manager who selects exactly which securities to include within the fund. When choosing which mutual fund to invest in, an investor will look at the underlying securities that the fund is invested in. They will then select the fund that best fits their investment goals. Investors will also check to see if the fund is actively managed or passively managed. The difference being that actively managed funds attempt to select specific securities to invest in and generate above market returns. They also charge higher fees on average. A passively managed fund typically tracks an index like the Dow Jones Industrial Average or S&P 500. They also have lower fees than the actively managed funds. **It should be noted that passively managed funds have been known to beat out actively managed funds over longer periods of time**. Think of a mutual fund as a basket of stocks, bonds, futures, or currencies that the portfolio manager has selected. When you buy into the mutual fund, you effectively buy into the entire selected portfolio as well.

Hedge Funds

A hedge fund is effectively a mutual fund with several key differences. To start, a hedge fund is not open to individual investors with a smaller net worth. Hedge funds are not open to the general public. In order to join a hedge fund, one must meet the minimum capital requirement of the hedge fund. The hedge fund minimum can range from $100,000 to $2,000,000. As you can see, hedge fund investors are in a different class from individual investors. The goal of a hedge fund is to bring above average market returns. Because of this goal, hedge funds have to be actively managed in order to attempt to beat out the market consistently year after year. Hedge funds often use high-risk methods in order to generate their above market returns. High-risk methods include short positions, option trading, and market arbitrage opportunity. In recent years, hedge funds have been accused of market manipulation with very little SEC intervention when it occurs.

Pension Funds

Pension funds are a type of fund that has gradually been decreasing in use in the corporate world. Most companies now offer a 401k match program rather than deal with the hassle of a pension fund. In simplified terms, a pension fund is an investment fund that pays for employee retirement commitments. Contributions to the fund are made by employees, employers, or both. The contributions made to the pension fund are invested on the employee's behalf and set aside for the employee's future benefit. Upon retirement, the employee receives an income source for them to use in retirement. While there are certain regulatory requirements for the funds such as a specified number of safe and risky assets and liquidity requirements, these regulations are not important to understanding that they are a type of institutional investor.

Insurance Companies

While a bit strange, insurance companies are also classified as institutional investors. The reason for this is that insurance companies will sell a policy to individuals. The individuals will then pay the insurance company premiums for the created policy. The insurance company then uses those payments to invest and create a source of capital to deal with future claims and to generate profit for themselves. Because insurance companies need to meet certain regulatory requirements and need to ensure that they have sufficient capital to meet a claim regardless of market volatility, insurance companies invest heavily into the bond market. That is not to say that they do not invest in the stock market at all, but the larger portion of their investments are placed into the bond market to better insulate themselves from unexpected market volatility.

Where are the Markets?

While the financial markets used to take place on trading floors where workers would shout buy and sell orders at each other while prices were updated manually, that is not the case today. Today, the markets are digital and electronic. There is no need to go to a specific floor to purchase a security. Buy and Sell orders can be executed from anywhere with an internet connection. This means that anyone in the world is capable of accessing and trading on the financial markets in today's environment. That being said, some of the financial markets operate within the time of their home environments. Which brings us to our next question.

When do the markets operate?

The time in which specific financial markets operate often depends on their geographic location. Some markets are considered to be global and operate 24/7 and others are based in specific countries and use their time zones to open and close the markets. Here we will show each of the markets to cover in this book, and we will explain which times they occupy in the market.

Stock Market

The stock market is a broad term which describes the buying and selling of a company's stock. In reality, there are many stock exchanges in other countries that perform similar functions that the New York Stock Exchange performs in the United States. The two largest stock exchanges in the world, however, are both located in the United States. The largest being the New York Stock Exchange (NYSE) and the second largest being the National Association of Securities Dealers Automated Quotations (NASDAQ). I know, it's a long name. We will use these two as an example. Both the NYSE and NASDAQ operate between the hours of 9:30 AM and 4:00 PM during the week. This excludes weekends and national holidays. Other exchanges have different hours of operation, and it is up to investors to know the times of their respective markets.

Bond Market

The bond market has many similarities to the stock market in the sense that several countries have their own systems and organized exchanges. The bond market for the NYSE is operated from 8:00 AM till 5:00 PM.

Money Market

The money market operates at the same time as the bond market.

Foreign Exchange Markets

The foreign exchange market focuses on the trading of foreign currency all across the world. As a result, the foreign exchange market is traded 24/7. Foreign currencies are traded across computers across several major exchanges. This means that someone is capable of trading foreign currencies at any point and time throughout the world. There are four major exchanges that split the work of the trading for the world time zones. The four major exchanges are Australia, Tokyo, London, and New York. Because of where the markets are located, there are several hours that overlap with each other in each market.

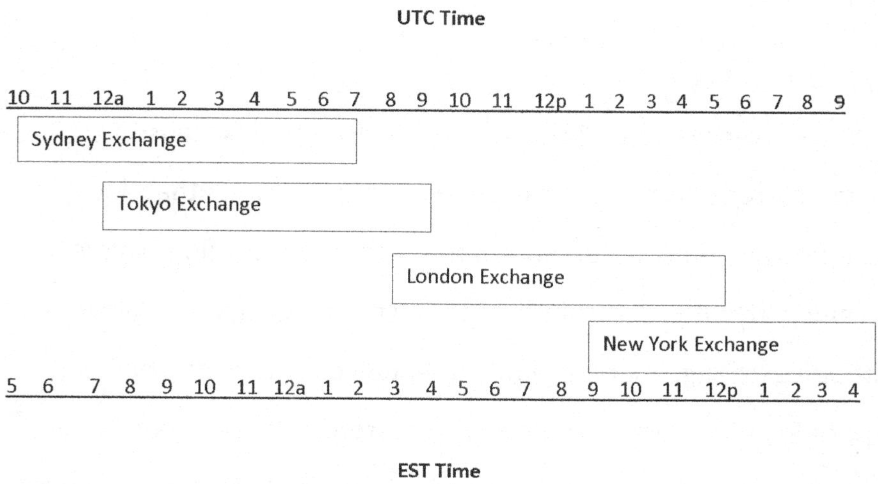

Forwards/Futures Market

The short answer for the futures market is that it depends on what futures you are currently trading. The market is also traded electronically which allows for trading to occur for 23 ½ hours every day from Sunday through Friday. Basically doing 24/6 trading. Most markets will open on Sunday at 6:00 PM and close at 5:00 PM on Friday. While futures markets still use pit trading, it has diminished in importance as electronic trading has become more popular.

Options Market

The option markets trade between the hours of 9:30 AM till 4:00 PM. While this is the time zone for the American markets, the times may differ depending on the specific market and country you are using to facilitate this trade. Each market sets its own times on when its assets are traded.

Cryptocurrency

Cryptocurrency trades 24/7. The reason for this is because cryptocurrency is run across a network of computers that does not require any human intervention to continue to function. This is significantly different from the foreign exchange market. While the foreign exchange market requires that an exchange be open and operational in order to trade, cryptocurrency does not need any specific exchange to be open in order to be traded. This is one way that cryptocurrency is able to function as a decentralized currency.

Why the Markets Exist?

After all this information, we finally come down to why the markets even exist in the first place. In this section, we can view this from two perspectives. The first perspective is that of the corporation.

A corporation operates in the non-financial market. They produce goods and services that are purchased and consumed by individuals. Eventually, a corporation may feel that they could expand if they only had additional capital. While they may be able to generate some of that capital from their profit, it is more advantageous to obtain that capital from investors. As a result, a corporation may issue a bond or stock to obtain capital. The first corporation to have this idea was the Dutch East India Company in 1602.

The Dutch East India Company was a massive conglomerate in its day that had a legal monopoly on trade with the East Indies. This legal monopoly was formed from a royal charter which granted them a 20-year monopoly. Eventually, investors would fund the voyages that the company took on in exchange for a portion of the profits. While risky, these can be thought of as the first "stock" that a company would issue in order to fund a project. Later on, the company would issue permanent shares of its company to investors. Meaning that the Dutch East India Company was the first company to sell ownership of its company in exchange for capital and a right to a portion of the profits. Eventually, the company would go on to issue bonds to fund new voyages rather than selling a portion of the future profit. In summary, the financial markets exist in part due to corporations requiring the use of additional capital and using investors as a means of obtaining it.

The second perspective on why the financial markets exist is that of the individual investor. The individual investor is typically someone who has obtained some degree of wealth. With that wealth, the investor requires a place to store it or put it to work. The financial markets attract investors who are looking to put their money to work. Investors can then pick and select the company or companies that they believe will provide them with the greatest return. It is interesting to note that investors would rather be exposed to risk of a market crash or company failure rather than be exposed to the natural devaluation of their chosen currency through inflation. Regardless, the financial markets also exist in part due to investors desiring some kind of return on their money.

As time has passed and markets become larger and more complex, the markets have standardized the way that securities are bought and sold. This makes it easier for buyers and sellers to become connected and trade capital for return. The financial markets have developed into an intermediary where companies and investors meet. When the project that the company is doing is funded, the investor will hopefully create a return on their investment based on how well the project does. In this sense, the markets were created to generate wealth for both companies and investors. With this system investors are given access to companies they normally would not be allowed to touch.

The main idea here is that the financial markets exist because investors need a place to put their money and companies need money in order to finance their activities. This has created one of the largest exchanges in the world and there does not seem to be an end in sight

2.

Equity Market

The Equity market is the simplest market to understand because of the way that it works. The equity markets are where buyers and sellers of stocks meet. These stocks have various prices and are valued in different ways. Before we understand how to value a stock, we need to understand what a stock is. In its simplest form, stock is partial ownership of a company. When you own a company's stock, you own the company. You may own a tiny portion of the company, but you do own the company.

This is an incredible opportunity for an individual to be able to own pieces of their favorite companies. If you buy 100 shares of Apple stock, then you own Apple. You own a very small portion of Apple, but you do own Apple. If you retain ownership of the company, you are eligible to receive a portion of that company's profit. If Apple posts a profit of $50 billion, they may choose to distribute a portion of those earnings to the shareholders. Because of this, stockholders may receive a reward for holding a stock which is referred to as a dividend.

While owning stocks and gaining access to their profits may entice individuals to join the markets, some people may be skeptical. If stocks are ownership, then does that mean that I am also liable for any debt that the company incurs? This is a valid concern, but it should not be a source of fear for fledgling investors. All publicly traded companies are set up as C corporations. This is a classification of a company that protects owners of the corporation from attacks on their personal assets. For example, assume that an Apple owner owns a $30,000 car. If Apple ever declared bankruptcy, the creditors could not go after the owner's car. The reason for this is that a C corporation protects owners from personal liability should a company ever become insolvent.

It should be noted that a company must be public in order to be purchased by the general public. Many companies are extremely valuable, but they are not publicly traded. Private companies typically have a smaller number of owners and investors, and they do not allow the general public to gain access to their corporation and business decisions. While a private company may be set up as a C corporation, they can also be set up as a sole proprietorship, partnership, S corporation, or a Limited Liability Corporation (LLC). For the purposes of the equity markets, we will assume that we are discussing a C corporation as they are the only corporate entity that can be publicly traded on an organized exchange.

Stock exchanges are set up all across the world, but the largest are based in the United States. The NYSE is currently the largest exchange in the world. In order to get listed on the NYSE, companies must meet several qualifications. Standard qualifications for an American-based company include a minimum of 400 shareholders who own at least 100 shares each, and at least 1.1 million shares of stock to trade. The market value of the shares must be at least $40 million. Stock price must be at least $4 dollars a share. A company must also have posted at least $10 million in pretax income for the past three years to be considered. Clearly, a company does not accidentally get listed on the NYSE. They must meet stringent requirements to even be considered. While a company may get successfully listed on the NYSE, how do individual investors go about purchasing stocks?

Individual investors work with brokerages that represent them in the markets. Broadly speaking, a broker is generally defined as "any person engaged in the business of effecting transactions in securities for the account of others." In English, brokers are entities who execute orders on behalf of the investors. When an investor asks to purchase a stock, the broker is the one who facilitates the transaction and ensures that it properly goes through. Brokers are subject to several laws and regulations to ensure that they do not participate in any illegal transactions.

To start, a broker must register with the Securities and Exchange Commission (SEC). Without an SEC registration, a broker is not allowed to trade on a national securities exchange. The most important regulations regarding brokers have to do with the wide potential for fraud to occur against investors. After all, brokers handle money on behalf of the investors. The potential for fraud is massive, and regulations help to ensure that there are not any problems with the way that brokers conduct their business. The most important regulations as it relates to investors are the "Duty of Fair Dealing", "Duty of Best Execution", "Customer Confirmation Rule", "Disclosure of Credit Terms", and "Restrictions on Insider Trading"

The Duty of Fair Dealing states that brokers will deal fairly with their customers. Specifically, this includes the "duties to execute orders promptly, disclose certain material information (*i.e.*, information the customer would consider important as an investor), charge prices reasonably related to the prevailing market, and fully disclose any conflict of interest."

The Duty of Best Execution states that a broker must obtain the best possible price for its customers. If a market price for security is between $49.50 and $49.75, the broker must attempt to execute the order at $49.50 if the customer is purchasing the stock. If selling the stock, the broker must attempt to execute the order at $49.75. Effectively, the broker must seek out and attempt to gain the most favorable terms for its customers under the current circumstances when the order is given.

The Customer Confirmation Rule requires that a broker must provide investors with specific information at or before a transaction takes place. Information includes the date, time, identity, price, and number of shares involved in a transaction. They must also disclose the capacity and compensation they require for executing a trade on your behalf. If they receive any third-party compensation for executing a trade, they must disclose the source of the third-party and the amount of compensation they are receiving. Additional information may be required to be disclosed to an investor depending on the broker's situation and if it could affect the investor's decision.

Disclosure of Credit Terms is required for any investors who purchase securities using credit. Some investors may borrow money in order to purchase securities. The broker is required to disclose the terms of borrowing that money to its customers.

Restrictions on Insider Trading is another requirement that bars the ability of individuals with material non-public information to purchase and sell stocks. This Act requires that brokers enforce written policies that are designed to prevent their employees from using this information for material gain. While this is not even close to a comprehensive list of all the regulations that brokerages have, these are several of the significant ones as they relate to investors.

Now that we understand that in order for individuals to purchase stocks they must go through a brokerage. We will discuss the types of stock that are available to purchase. In general, there are two different types of stocks to purchase on the market, common stock and preferred stock. Additionally, stocks are typically divided into more categories that describe how they tend to act and respond in different markets.

Common Stock

When someone says that they own shares of company, they are typically referring to the purchase of common stock. Common stock is the most prevalent form of shares sold and purchased in the equity markets. Hence the name "common" stock. Common stock is eligible to receive dividends from a company and are also given voting rights on business decisions. Dividends can vary and are not guaranteed. If a company is running into difficult times, they may cut off the regular dividend payments in order to keep the company running. Common stock price is also more volatile and subject to large price swings. This indicates that there is more risk, but there is also the potential for higher long-term returns.

Preferred Stock

Preferred stock is the second type of stock available to purchase on the market. It is much less prevalent and has decreased in popularity as time has passed. This is because most companies would rather issue bonds than issue preferred stock. The benefit of preferred stock over common stock is access to preferred dividends. Dividends are usually higher than common stock and are guaranteed. Meaning that preferred stockholders are guaranteed to receive dividend payments even if payments are cut off for common stockholders. Dividends are also paid to preferred stockholders first before common stockholders in the event of a bankruptcy. These attributes mean that the price of preferred stock is less volatile than common stock. While this is beneficial when a company is performing poorly, it also means that the price of preferred stock will not increase nearly as quickly when the company is performing well. Preferred stockholders typically do not have voting rights, but there are exceptions.

In chart form,

	Preferred Stock	Common Stock
Pros	• Dividends are fixed and are often higher than dividends given to common stock. • Less volatility in share price • More likely to recover some part of the investment during a bankruptcy	• Much larger potential for return in the long-term if the company does well • Voting rights and a voice in making decisions
Cons	• No voting rights • Lower potential for growth when a company is doing well	• Dividends are typically lower if they are even offered • Much more volatile due to the lack of consistent and regular income and higher degree of risk • Most likely to lose investment if company declares a bankruptcy
Goals	Great for investors looking for long-term **income**	Great for investors looking for long-term **growth and profit**

Companies will also divide their stock into different classifications. Class names can be anything that the company decides, but typically they are divided into Class A or Class B shares. Classes are usually distinct and have different characteristics for each class. Some classes of shares may hold more voting power over company decisions than other classes of shares. A great example for a complicated class structure would be the way that Google classifies their shares to investors.

Google has three classifications for their shares. Google has Class A, Class B, and Class C shares. Google's complicated class structure came about when the company founders looked for a solution to issuing as many shares of the company while also maintaining control of the company. This was the solution they came up with to achieve both goals.

Class A shares are publicly available stock that can be purchased by investors. These shares all have the standard **one** vote per share of stock. Class B shares are not publicly available for investors to purchase and are owned by Google insiders and are each worth **ten** votes each. This solves Google's problem about retaining control of their company, but what was the purpose of the Class C shares? The class C shares were created on April 2014. They were created after Google decided to perform a stock split on the Class A shares and create a brand-new class of shares. The Class C shares were created with the same intent as the Class A shares with one notable difference. The Class C shares **do not** have any voting rights. While this was a controversial move at the time, it is the way that Google has chosen to operate their business. Hopefully this serves as an excellent example of different stock classes and why they are relevant.

While stock types and classes are official terms for different forms of stock on the market, there are also informal terms that investors use to describe the way that certain stocks tend to behave. Those informal terms are company size, industry, location, and style.

Company Size: Company size has nothing to do with the physical size of the company. Instead, it refers to the market capitalization of the company. Other investors may refer to this as the total value of the company. The three main categories of company size are large-cap, mid-cap, and small-cap. Large-cap companies have a market capitalization of $10 billion or more. Mid-cap companies have a market capitalization between $2 billion and $10 billion, and small-cap companies have a market capitalization between $300 million and $2 billion.

Industry: Company stocks are often referred to by the industry where they conduct their business. For example, a popular industry is energy. Energy stocks are companies that are involved in the production, transportation, or sale of energy products. These products can include electricity, oil, or gasoline. Using this naming method can help an investor to understand what the core of the business likely is before any preliminary research is conducted. Other popular industries include real estate, consumer staples, and healthcare.

Location: While this is a less used description, it is used enough to warrant a quick description. Stocks can also be grouped by geographic location. Stocks are often classified as being from the United States, international, or an emerging market. For the purposes in this book, we will refer to stocks as either from the United States or international.

Style: Generally, there are three styles to use when describing a stock. The first is value. When someone mentions a value stock, they are stating that they believe the stock is undervalued. The investor believes that the company is worth a lot more, or that the company will do extremely well in the future. When an investor says this, they believe that the stock is currently overlooked by the market, but it will do well in the future. The second style of stock is growth. Growth stocks are stocks that are growing very rapidly, and the stock's price is rapidly outperforming the overall market. Typically, these stocks are growing very aggressively and the price increases day after day. Because these companies are focused on expansion, they will usually have a small dividend yield or not post a dividend at all. The reasoning behind this is that the company is focusing its resources on growing rather than giving their profits back to their investors. The third style of stock are dividend stocks. Dividend stocks are stocks that consistently and regularly post a dividend to their shareholders. Investors will purchase shares of these companies when they are looking for an established company that will provide them with a certain degree of income.

What moves a stock's price?

The answer to this question is simple. If a stock is purchased more than it is sold on a given day, it goes up. If a stock is sold more than it is bought on a given day, it goes down. Stock price is completely controlled by the supply and demand on the financial markets. If you were expecting a more complicated answer, I'm sorry. It really is that simple.

Buying and Selling a stock

Now that we know what moves a stock, what do we have to do in order to purchase one? The first step would be to register with a brokerage and provide them with your information. Once you are approved, you can give orders to your brokerage. Your brokerage is your equipment, your dollars are your soldiers, and you are the general. Much like a real army, you need to give your soldiers orders to execute. Each order is different and will cause a different effect. Below are several orders that are commonly used in stock trading.

Market Order: A market order is the simplest order on the market. A market order will execute immediately at the current market price. These orders are typically the quickest and fastest. Additionally, these orders are guaranteed to execute because the broker will attempt to fill the order as quickly as possible. If dollars are soldiers, then this order is a blitz. Your dollars are charging to obtain as many shares of a stock as possible before you run out of men.

Limit Order: A limit order is used when an investor wants to buy or sell a stock at a specific price. This order will only execute at the price that the investor sets. The investor sets the minimum or maximum price to buy or sell. Here, your soldiers are waiting to ambush. They will only move based on what the current market price is and whatever price the general has set. Generally, there are four types of limit orders.

Types of Limit Orders	
Buy Limit	A buy limit is used when an investor wants to purchase a security at or below a price. The investor likely feels that the current stock price is too high and would rather purchase the stock at a lower price. The investor proceeds to place the order at a price lower than the current market price.
Buy Stop	A buy stop is the opposite of a buy limit. The investor wants to purchase the security at a price that is higher than the current market price. While this seems like an extremely strange thing to do, it is usually used to cover short positions (more on that below) and when investors expect the stock to continue rising in price. If the stock price breaks the set limit, then the order converts into a market order and is executed as quickly as possible.
Sell Limit	A sell limit is used when an investor would like to sell a stock at a specific price. The investor believes the stock price is too low or that it is not worth it to sell it at the current level. The investor sets the limit price above the current market price in this situation.
Sell stop	A sell stop is similar to a buy stop in that it seems like an irrational decision. A sell stop sets the selling price of a stock at a price below the current market price. If it reaches the set level, it also converts into a market order and is executed immediately. This order is used to limit potential losses or to protect a profit and ensure that an investor is able to make money. This is one of the most useful limit orders to help ensure that an investor leaves a trade at a profit. When a sell stop is used in this way, it is referred to as a stop loss order.

Short selling: A short sale is a way that an investor can make money on a stock when the price goes down. This is also referred to as a short position or short. To execute a short sale, an investor first decides on which stock they feel will perform badly in the future. They then go to their broker and state that they would like to short a specific stock. The broker lends the investor the desired number of shares. The investor then immediately sells the shares on the open market. If the price goes down, the investor buys the shares at the new current price and returns the shares back to the brokerage. This works because the brokerage did not lend the money in order to purchase the shares, instead they lent the shares to the investor. This means that the investor must return the exact number of shares to the brokerage. The shares may have gone up or down in value, but that does not change what was borrowed and must be returned. This is a **risky** order because the potential loss on an investment like this is considered to be **unlimited**. The maximum profit, however, is only **double**. If a company is financially weakening, short positions may be opened to capitalize on a drop in the share price. Short positions are also opened when investors would like to hedge their risk in the stock market.

Here is an example of a short position. I may view a stock that is priced at $700 per share. I can enter into a short position for 150 shares with my brokerage. The broker gives me 150 shares with a total value of $105,000. I then sell those shares on the market and receive $105,000 in cash. At this point, there are two scenarios that can occur. The stock price can go up or down. For simplicity, let's assume that the price will either drop or increase by $100.

Scenario 1

In the first scenario, the stock price **drops** by $100. This makes the market value of each stock $600. At this point the investor can close the account and take a profit. The investor then repurchases 150 shares at $90,000. The shares are returned to the brokerage, and the investor takes a **profit** of $105,000 minus $90,000. The total profit on the trade equals $15,000.

Scenario 2

In the second scenario, the stock price **rises** by $100. This makes the market value of each stock $800. At this point the investor can close the account and take a loss or keep the account open and risk further loss. Assuming that the investor chooses to close the account and take the loss, the investor then repurchases 150 shares at $120,000. The shares are returned to the brokerage, and the investor takes a **loss** of $120,000 minus $105,000. The total loss on the trade equals $15,000.

Other Stock Order Types

Below is a list of uncommon stock order types that are used in specific situations.

Good-Till-Cancelled Order

A GTC order is used to keep different orders open for a longer period of time. This type of order will remain active until the investor decides to cancel it. Brokerages typically limit the amount of time that an order can be active. Investors should check with their brokerages to see how long GTC orders are allowed to remain active.

Immediate or Cancel

An IOC order is an order that must be executed immediately. Brokerages typically execute these order types in mere seconds. Any portion of the order that is not filled during the execution is cancelled. If an IOC order comes in for 10,000 shares and only 420 shares can be executed, then the remaining 9,580 shares are cancelled. Additionally, if no shares can be executed then the entire order is cancelled.

All or None

An AON order is used to specify the exact number of shares to be purchased or else the order will fail to execute. If there are not enough available shares to be purchased, then the order will wait until enough available shares appear and the order can be completed in its entirety. Pretend that an investor places and order for 6,970 shares and only 6,969 shares are available for purchase. The order will not execute until 6,970 shares can be purchased at once.

Fill or Kill

An FOK order is a combination of an IOC and AON order. A FOK order must meet several conditions in order to execute. The order must be executed within a few seconds and the entirety of the order must be executed. If the order is not immediately executed or the desired number of shares are not available, then the order will cancel.

Day Order

If an order is not specifically requested as a GTC order, then it will be listed as a day order. A day order must be executed during the day that it is ordered. If it does not execute, then the order will cancel and must be reopened the next day.

Margin

Before moving on to discuss other topics, we need to briefly discuss margin and how it works. The reason being that it is an extremely fundamental topic that will come up in later chapters. Some brokerages may allow their investors to use margin accounts. A margin account is an account where the broker will lend money to investors in order to make their trades. This is an extremely widespread practice and popular with speculative traders. Margin increases the purchasing power of investors, but it can also result in larger than normal losses for traders. Ultimately, it involves borrowing money in order to make investments. This leads to situations where investors will have to pay back the money that they borrowed. Because of the risky nature of these accounts, they are highly regulated and controlled.

Currently, the Securities and Exchange Commission (SEC) requires that investors post an initial margin and maintain a level of equity in the account to be allowed to trade on margin. The **initial margin** is the total amount that you can borrow when entering into a trade. The minimum initial margin amount is 50% of the purchase price of the securities you are buying. After you post the initial margin and own the securities, you must maintain a **maintenance margin** in the account. The maintenance margin minimum is 25% of the total market value of securities that were purchased on margin. It should be noted that brokers can have higher margin requirements for their accounts. A broker may require a higher initial margin and maintenance margin. Typically, maintenance margins are at least 30% to 40% for most brokers. If the balance in your account falls below the maintenance margin, you will receive a **margin call**. In a margin call, the broker will ask the client to place additional funds into the account, or the account will be immediately closed out.

The way that the maintenance margin is calculated is not to the benefit of the investor. This is because the maintenance margin is based on the total equity that you have left in the account. It does not take into account the borrowed funds that were used. Here is an example of this occurring. Let's say that an individual purchases $20,000 worth of securities and they put in $10,000 cash and borrow the rest on margin. This way they meet the 50% initial margin requirement. Additionally, let's assume that the broker requires a maintenance margin of 40%.

$20,000 value of securities

$10,000 cash

$10,000 money given on margin

After this point, the value of the purchased securities drops by 20%

$16,000 value of securities

$6,000 cash

$10,000 money given on margin

Maintenance margin = equity in the account/current value of securities

Maintenance margin = 6,000/16,000 = 37.5%

At this point, the investor would be receiving a margin call because they have gone below the required maintenance margin for this broker.

As a side note, it is clear to see that trading on margin can be a risky endeavor. In addition to risking a larger loss than the initial investment, there is usually interest that is charged to the investor for borrowing the margin funds. Meaning that if you make a profit or loss, you will be paying interest on the funds that you borrowed from the brokerage. Lastly, it should be noted that a short selling order is always traded on a margin account. The reason for this is that an investor is borrowing shares of a company and they must meet an initial margin before the brokerage will be able to confirm the order.

Corporate Actions

Companies that are listed on a publicly traded exchange are able to issue corporate actions. Corporate actions are actions that corporations use to change and control the stock price. As an investor, it is extremely important to understand how these actions can affect you. Lastly, corporate actions can be used to understand the health and future of a corporation. Investors will often respond differently depending on the corporate action that the company is undergoing. Below is a list of corporate actions that companies can use to manipulate their stock price.

Stock Split: A stock split is a common occurrence in the corporate world and is very simple to understand. This event is used to lower the price of shares. A stock split divides the value of each share of the company, increases the total number of shares, and reduces the price of the shares by the divided amount. An extremely common stock split is a two-for-one stock split. During a two-for-one stock split, a company's stock doubles, and the price of the stock is split in half. If an investor had 100 shares of a company at $50 per share, now they have 200 shares of the same company at $25 per share. A company can choose to do this action at any ratio. Meaning that three-for-one and ten-for-one stock splits are not uncommon and do occur. When a stock split occurs, it often indicates to investors that a company is doing well. As a result, the share price may immediately increase after a stock split has occurred.

Reverse Stock Split: Remember a stock split? This is the opposite of a stock split and is used when a company wants to increase the price of its shares. A reverse stock split multiplies the value of each share, increases the price of shares by the multiplied amount, and divides the number of shares. For example, assume a company chooses to undergo a five-for-one reverse stock split. If you owned 100 shares of a company at $50 per share, you now own 20 shares at $250 per share. Just like a stock split, a company can choose to undergo this action at any ratio. When a reverse stock split occurs, it often indicates to investors that a company is doing poorly. As a result, the share price may decrease after a reverse stock split because investors believe the company may be in trouble.

Dividends: Dividends are an extremely widespread practice and many companies undergo this action on a quarterly basis. While many companies schedule their dividends in advance, it is not necessary and dividend distribution can be erratic and unpredictable. Ultimately, dividends are a portion of the company's profits that are being given back to shareholders. Many investors will purchase a stock simply because they have a strong record of paying dividends to their investors. A regular and consistent dividend can reduce the risk of a sudden and rapid decrease in stock price. There are five types of dividends that a company can undergo.

The first dividend is a cash dividend. This is the most common dividend. **Whenever this book refers to a dividend, it is referring to this type of dividend.** A cash dividend is the simplest one to understand. The company simply declares a specific amount of money that they will distribute per share. If a company declares that each share will receive a dividend of $0.75 per share, then each owner will be paid $0.75 for each share of the company that they own. If you own 100 shares of a company, then you will receive $75.

The second dividend is a stock dividend. It is similar to a cash dividend, but instead of cash, investors receive company stock. Assume a shareholder owns 10 shares and a stock dividend of 10% is declared. The shareholder will receive one additional share of the company for every ten that is owned.

The third dividend is a property dividend. A property dividend is considered to be any non-monetary asset that is given to its investors. A property dividend can literally be anything that a company wants. While these types of dividends are rare, they can be interesting. Usually they are used for tax reduction purposes, but they do not have to be. For example, say that a baseball company has several million unsold signed baseballs of a nonpopular player in their inventory. The company could sell the assets to recover the loss, or they could distribute the signed baseballs to their shareholders as a property dividend.

The fourth dividend is a scrip dividend. A scrip dividend occurs when a company does not have enough funds to pay a scheduled dividend. The company may choose to issue a scrip dividend instead. A scrip dividend is effectively an IOU to pay the dividend at a future date. This type of dividend is extremely rare as most companies will simply not pay a dividend if they are unable to.

Lastly, we have the fifth dividend which is a liquidating dividend. This dividend is also rarely used and occurs when a company is either partially or completely shutting down. The company will sell as many of its assets as it possibly can and then issue the remaining cash to shareholders after paying off any debts it may have had. Even if a company is shutting down, they will likely never use this type of dividend.

Merger: A merger occurs when two or more companies decide to combine into one new entity. During a merger, all companies are in agreement and are on friendly terms. Usually, one company will surrender its stock to another. Mergers rarely occur, however, without one business giving money to the other business in order to facilitate the merger. The reason being that the two companies are rarely on the same footing. Typically, one company will pay to combine with the other company before a merger officially occurs. For example, Company A could agree to pay $20 per share of Company B. After the merger occurs, Company B shareholders receive $20 and the shares would be delisted as Company C is formed. Mergers affect stock prices positively or negatively. The changes in stock price are based on whether or not investors feel that the new merger will positively or negatively impact the business.

Acquisitions: Acquisitions are similar to mergers with several key differences. During an acquisition, the two companies do not come together to form a new entity. Acquisitions can also be friendly, but they can also be unfriendly. During an acquisition, a company purchases a majority stake in another company's shares. A majority stake is ownership of 51% or more of another company. In this case, the purchased company's shares may remain on the market and other investors will not be given a payout during the acquisition. After that point, one company owns another company and are able to make decisions on their behalf. There are two types of acquisitions. If an acquisition is friendly, it is very similar to a merger. Both companies get together and decide what they are going to do. This is very common when a public company acquires a private company. The reason for this is that a private company has all the power to decide whether to sell to the public company. The other type of acquisition is not friendly. This type of acquisition is referred to as a hostile takeover. When a hostile takeover occurs, one company will aggressively purchase as many shares of another company as possible until they obtain 51% or more of the shares of the company. When this occurs, an attacked firm may quickly realize that another entity has the power to do anything.

Acquisitions are different from mergers, but they both go hand in hand when a firm is attempting to expand by using another company.

Reverse Merger: Interestingly enough, a reverse merger is not a merger. A reverse merger is an acquisition that occurs when a private company attempts to take over a public company. Typically, the public company is doing poorly, and the private company is looking for ways to expand their business. A private company may also undergo this process because of the fact that this acquisition transforms the private company into a publicly traded company. Through this method, a private company becomes a public company without going through the tedious initial public offering process. The private company can even change their name and issue shares to the public without any of the normal initial requirements and approval.

Spin-off: A spin-off is an action that companies use when they are attempting to establish a new independent entity. A public company will sell some assets or distribute new shares in order to establish a new company. The new shares are usually offered to existing shareholders before they are offered to new investors.

Tender Offer: A tender offer is an offer by an entity to purchase shares of a company at a premium. A tender offer is a public offer to invite shareholders to sell shares at a set price and time. If a company's stock is trading for $5 per share, a tender offer may tell investors that they are willing to purchase shares for $8 per share. Tender offers will often have stipulations before the trade goes through. One stipulation that is often used is that 51% or more shares must accept the tender offer or else the trade will cancel. There are usually two reasons why a tender offer is used. The first is when a company that would like to acquire another company issues a tender offer to existing shareholders. This tender offer is an expensive way to acquire a firm, but it can help in locking in the trade by enticing shareholders to sell their shares at a premium. A tender offer can also be issued by the existing firm in order to avoid a potential hostile takeover in the future. Again, this is an expensive defense, but some firms may find the action to be worth the extra protection.

Corporate Buy-Back: A corporate buy back occurs when a company is doing well financially, but the firm's stock price seems to continue going down. While a tender offer is buying stocks at a premium, a corporate buy back is when a corporation purchases its own shares on the open market at the fair value price. This decision may be viewed negatively among the corporation's shareholders. After all, if a company has so much extra money lying around, why would they not dividend that income to shareholders or attempt to expand further? Other investors may take it as a good sign that the company is strong enough to buy back its own shares. Regardless, it is an action that occurs when a company believes that their stock price is undervalued, and the company is doing extremely well.

Leveraged Buyout: A leveraged buyout is the acquisition of another company using a large amount of borrowed funds. Typically, the buyout uses 90% debt and 10% equity to finance the cost of the acquisition. This is considered to be a hostile takeover, but it uses the assets of the target company as collateral for the loan. LBO's can be risky and often fall through or lead to the bankruptcy of the target corporation after it is unable to meet the terms of the loan used to acquire it. Think about it, another company obtains a loan from an investment bank to acquire your company and they use your assets and cash flow as collateral for the loan. It would be funny if it wasn't for the fact that it is a real event that does occur. It is almost like obtaining a loan to buy someone else's house and then using the items that are in their house as collateral for the loan if the house has financial problems. Regardless of its strange nature, a leveraged buyout is used when somebody wants to take a public corporation and turn it into a private corporation. Leveraged buyouts are also used to spin off a portion of the existing company or to transfer private property to another owner. A famous example of a leveraged buyout occurred when Dell computers decided to take their company from public to private. The reasoning behind this decision was that Dell was under the influence of too many investors that were not focused on growth. Instead, the investors were attempting to drain the company until it went out of business. By using a leveraged buyout, Dell was able to go private and eventually reverted back into a public company that was stronger than ever.

Determining Value

Now that we understand the basic terms that the stock market uses, we can discuss what investors spend time researching when making investing decisions. The primary focus of most analysts and investors is the value of the company. Specifically, they want to understand whether the company is correctly valued by the market. In this area, there is immense debate and discussion as different people have different opinions on specific companies.

In the stock market, there are two sides. One side believes the stock price will increase, and the other believes the price will decrease. The beauty of the stock market is that **both sides think they are right.** In this, there is immense debate as to the value of a stock and the value that it will provide in the future. Analysts must select stocks that they believe have the ability to perform well in the market in the future and sustain an advantage for years to come. When investors discuss value, they are attempting to understand if a company is undervalued, properly valued, or overvalued.

If a company is undervalued, an investor believes that the stock is currently trading at a price that is lower than what the company is currently worth or will be worth in the future. An undervalued security can lead to an incredible return in the future if the investor's belief is correct. By the time that other investors realize what the stock is worth, it will have already increased in price and the investor who purchased when the stock was undervalued will receive a sizeable "reward" for their prediction.

When a company is properly valued, an investor believes that the stock is currently trading at a fair price. An investment at this time may be a worthwhile investment but should only produce a decent return over time. At this price, the company is trading at a price that is consistent with the overall sentiment the market has towards the company's profitability now and in the future. In reality, few investors ever believe that a stock is trading at its fair value.

When a company is overvalued, an investor believes that the stock is currently trading at a price that is higher than the company is actually worth. If an investor believes that a stock is overvalued, they will avoid purchasing the company because they believe that the price is higher than the company should be worth. Whether a company is overvalued, properly valued, or undervalued is a matter of opinion for investors. The investor will eventually be proven right or wrong by the market.

As it relates to value, there are two theories that can help us better understand how stock price changes are viewed by investors. It will also help you understand that investors have absolutely no clue what they are doing when determining a stock's fair price, and they have no clue whether a stock's price will increase or decrease. The first theory is the efficient market hypothesis. This theory states that we must assume that markets are efficient. This means that a stock price is always at its fair value on the market. This is because the stock price perfectly reflects all information that investors currently have available. This theory believes that it is impossible to purchase undervalued securities and sell them later because the stock price is always properly valued. This theory is heavily disputed by anyone with a brain. While the theory may work over long periods of time, the theory fails to work in even the slightest sense on a short-term basis. The reason being that stocks are undervalued or overvalued on a daily basis.

Additionally, this theory states that it is impossible for investors to beat the market on a long-term basis by purchasing undervalued securities. If someone does beat the market it is due to luck and not actual skill. Naturally, we can take our eyes off of our textbooks and understand that investors do exist that have beaten the market on a consistent basis by purchasing undervalued stocks. While the theory does give some good advice, such as investing money into low cost mutual funds and ETF's, overall it is a theory that does not work as often as its promoters would like. As a result, the semi-strong efficiency and weak efficiency market theory were developed to better explain irregularities in the market.

The second theory to understand the way that a stock price moves is the random walk theory. This theory is also referred to as the drunken man theory. This theory states that it is impossible to predict whether a stock price will go up or down on a daily basis. Similar to a drunk person walking, you never know whether they will step to the left or the right. The stock price moves in a similar fashion and is impossible to predict. Additionally, because the stock price movement is random, past movements cannot be used to predict future movements. This is why investors should focus on the potential long-term results of a company rather than the short-term. This theory also concludes that there is too much irregularity in individual stocks. That is why investors would be better off matching the market using an index fund rather than individually choosing stocks based on their personal opinion.

On a side note, an author named Burton Malkiel actually wrote a book on random walk theory and used it to promote the efficient market hypothesis. The book actually said that a blindfolded monkey throwing darts at a dart board could produce a portfolio that would perform just as well as a portfolio carefully created and crafted by experts. The book was published in 1973. In 1988, the "monkey theory" was tested. The Wall Street Journal used staffers as "monkeys" and had them throw darts at a dart board to create a portfolio. They created 140 randomly selected portfolios and compared them with professional portfolios created by experts. The experts won 87 contests and the dart throwers won 55. Additionally, only 76 of the expert's portfolios actually outperformed the Dow Jones that year. Because expert portfolios only beat the general market a little over half the time, it was concluded that investors would be better off investing in a passive fund that charged lower fees than a fund managed by experts.

Another fun monkey story occurred when CEO Rob Arnett of Research Affiliates stated that "the monkeys have done a much better job than both the experts and the stock market." The company created 100 portfolios of 30 randomly selected stocks from a pool of 1,000 stocks. They created the portfolios every year from 1964 to 2010. On average, 98 out of the 100 "monkey portfolios" beat out the pool of 1,000 stocks every year. These results were explained by the higher likelihood of these portfolios to contain small-cap stocks. Because small-cap stocks are more volatile, they are much more likely to have larger returns than large-cap stocks. Because there were more small-caps than large-caps in the stock pool, it increased the likelihood of a small-cap being selected for a portfolio. Regardless, it was interesting to see that random stock picking produced significantly better returns over long periods of time when compared to the expert portfolios.

If this doesn't help show that stock experts and large funds do not know which way the market will turn, I don't know what will. At the end of this long explanation, hopefully you will understand that what investors believe to be overvalued and undervalued is a matter of opinion and that even Wall Street "experts" do not know what the future will be.

*skip this section if you are not interested in how investors determine a company's value *

What Investors Use to Determine Value

Now that we understand that stock valuations are a matter of opinion. What do investors use to form and develop those opinions? Investors will often use ratios and company financial information to decide whether a company is worth an investment. The reality is that these are ultimately theories that must be tested in the real world. In fact, all the technical analysis in the world cannot predict when a rapid rise or fall in stock price will occur. Additionally, stock pickers cannot predict the future and how the business environment will change over time. Regardless, investors can use past performance to predict future results and there are several items that they use to do exactly that.

One of the first things that investors look for when determining whether a stock is a buy are a company's financial statements. There are four main financial statements that are prepared for a company. The financial statements are the income statement, statement of retained earnings, balance sheet, and statement of cash flows. While I am not going to go into detail for each of these financial statements, I will explain which ones are the most important. Typically, the balance sheet and the income statement are the most used during analysis. The statement of cash flows is also used, but less importance is usually placed on it. It should be noted that all public companies are required to publish these statements.

An income statement is very easy to understand. In an income statement, a company's income and expenses are listed. The ultimate result is the net income. Net income is the amount of income left over after expenses. A standard income statement looks similar to this.

Income statement

	Year ended December 31, 2020
Revenue	**$45,000,000.00**
Cost of goods sold	$10,000,000.00
Gross Profit	**$35,000,000.00**
Selling, general, and administrative expense	$5,000,000.00
Research and Development	$2,000,000.00
Earnings before interest taxes and depreciation (EBITDA)	**$28,000,000.00**
Depreciation and amortization	$4,000,000.00
Earnings before interest and taxes (EBIT)	**$24,000,000.00**
Interest expense	$2,000,000.00
Income tax expense	$3,000,000.00
Net Income	**$19,000,000.00**

Next up, we have a balance sheet. A balance sheet lists all of the assets and liabilities that a company currently has. Balance sheets can be extremely complicated once previous years begin to be displayed together. For a simple example, we will use a balance sheet from one year. Next, we will look at the financial ratios that investors use to make their decisions. While this is certainly not a comprehensive list of the common financial ratics, I will briefly explain the ratios that are almost always used when initially analyzing a company.

Company ABC
Balance Sheet
December 31, 2020

Assets			**Liabilities**		
Current Assets			Current Liabilities		
Cash	$	4,800	Notes Payable	$	8,000
Petty Cash		300	Accounts Payable		227,900
Temporary Investments		500	Wages Payable		7,200
Account receivables – net		68,000	Interest Payable		3,100
Inventory		28,000	Taxes Payable		7,200
Supplies		4,500	Warranty Liability		2,100
Prepaid Insurance		2,200	Unearned Revenues		1,600
Total Current Assets		108,300	**Total Current Liabilities**		257,100
Investments		42,000			
			Long-Term Liabilities		
Property, Plant, and Equipment			Notes Payable		32,000
Land		5,750	Bonds Payable		280,000
Land Improvements		10,500	**Total Long-Term Liabilities**		312,000
Buildings		200,000			
Equipment		305,000			
Less: accum depreciation		(72,000)			
Prop, Plant, and Equipment		449,250	**Total Liabilities**		569,100
Intangible Assets			**Stockholders' Equity**		
			Common Stock		132,000
Trade Names		150,000	Retained Earnings		185,000
Total Intangible Assets		150,000	Less: Treasury Stock		(131,550)
Other Assets		5,000	**Total Stockholders' Equity**		185,450
Total Assets		$754,550	**Total Liabilities and Stockholders' Equity**		$754,550

In general, there are four types of ratios that investors use when evaluating a company for an investment. These ratios all explore a different aspect of a company's financial statements and allow investors to compare companies against each other.

Valuation Ratios

These ratios can be used to understand exactly what earnings the market believes a company will generate in the future. Investors use these ratios to determine what a company's current valuation is. These ratios are often affected by market sentiment toward a specific company and how much investors believe in a company's future. At the end of this section, a chart will be provided showing how to calculate all of these ratios.

EPS Ratio: The earnings per share ratio is a ratio to understand how much of a company's profits are divided among all the outstanding shares in the market. The earnings per share measures the net income that is earned on each share of stock that an investor purchased. This ratio is obtained by dividing net income (income statement) by the weighted average of shares outstanding. Weighted average is used because some shares of the company may not be publicly available for purchase.

P/E Ratio: This ratio is used to determine the price of each share of a company versus the earnings per share. In short, this ratio most accurately reflects the overall sentiment that the market has towards this company's future earnings. The higher the P/E ratio the more confident that investors are in a company's future. The reality, however, is that the higher the P/E ratio the less money that the company generates in proportion to its current share price. Investors are willing to pay steeper prices if they believe that the company will have future earnings to compensate for the higher share price. To calculate the P/E ratio, we get the current share price and divide it by the EPS ratio that we calculated above. This is considered to be one of the most important ratios to use when evaluating a company.

PEG Ratio: The PEG ratio is a continuation of the P/E ratio. The P/E ratio lacks the ability to predict future growth as it is used as an indicator of the current market sentiment. The PEG ratio attempts to rectify the problem by adding in future growth as a factor. To calculate the PEG ratio, divide the P/E ratio by the current earnings growth rate. The earnings growth rate is obtained by dividing the earnings in one year by the earnings in the previous year.

P/B Ratio: This is a seldom used ratio, but it is extremely common among more pessimistic investors. This ratio is used when attempting to compare what the current price of the stock is versus the book value of its assets. Book value is the value of assets as they are listed on the balance sheet. This is distinct from the market value of assets. The market value of an asset on the balance sheet can be higher or lower than the book value of those same assets. As a result, the ratio is used by investors that are analyzing a company's assets in relation to its stock price.

P/S Ratio: This ratio is used to determine how much investors are willing to pay for a stock for each dollar of sales. This ratio uses the past 12 months of sales when it is being calculated. This ratio is useful, but it does not take into account whether or not the company is even turning a profit. It ignores debt and expenses and only focuses on revenues. The lower this ratio is the more sales that are being generated compared to the company's share price.

Profitability Ratios

These ratios are used when investors want to analyze how profitable a company currently is. This is because a company may have high revenues, but too many expenses to turn a profit. All of these ratios are used to analyze profitability from several different angles.

Gross Margin: This ratio is used to analyze the margin that a company has for each product that it sells. This ratio uses **cost of goods sold** and not all expenses. The reason for this is that an investor wants to know the amount of cushion or margin that a company has to work with when bringing their product to market. Cost of goods sold includes all of the direct costs associated with producing a product. This includes direct labor costs and the cost of materials used during manufacturing. This does not include advertising and administrative expenses. Those are considered to be separate expenses that the remaining gross margin is used on. If a company has poor gross margin, it will be difficult for them to properly advertise their product before running out of money.

Operating Margin: This ratio is designed to show how much profit a company makes after deducting their variable costs. Variable costs include wages and raw materials. Operating margin is calculated without subtracting interest or tax expenses. The higher this margin is, the better a company is at being efficient and generating a profit.

Net Profit Margin: The net profit margin is used to show how much profit a company earns. Here, net income is divided by the total revenue of the firm. Then that number is multiplied by 100 to obtain a percentage. This leads to an exact amount of profit that the company has generated in a percentage form. This is one of the most important ratios to track when evaluating how well a company is performing.

ROE: Return on equity is a ratio that is used by current investors to see how their investment has performed over time. This does not actually indicate whether or not they have made or lost money for this investment. For this ratio, we get the net income of the company and subtract any preferred dividends. Then we divide that number by the shareholder's equity (balance sheet).

ROA: Return on assets is used to indicate a company's profitability in relation to their total assets. The higher the ROA the better that a company is doing in relation to its total assets. This ratio helps to show how well a company is doing in relation to the assets that they have purchased as an investment. This is useful because it does not penalize the company if they spend more money on equipment when building their business. The only thing that is important is how much income they were able to generate in proportion to the assets that they invested in.

ROI: This ratio is used after an investment or project. With this ratio, investors can understand how profitable an investment was. An ROI can be both negative and positive. Return on investment is also best used to evaluate specific projects that a company attempts to undergo. After a project has been completed the company can evaluate the project and better understand whether it was the correct decision.

Liquidity Ratios

Liquidity ratios are the best ratios to use to understand what would happen to a company if they needed to repay their debts. These are great ratios that are often used by debt investors and investors that are concerned about a potential bankruptcy. These ratios will usually analyze what a company would do if they had to cover an unexpected expense. For example, a massive factory might be a great asset, but a bank will not accept the factory equipment as payment for a loan. Using these ratios help investors have a clear understanding of a firm's financial position.

Current Ratio: The current ratio is a measure of how well a company can repay any debts that would be due within one year. Because of this, liquidity ratios usually analyze current assets and current liabilities. Any asset or liability that is "current" is to be collected or paid within one year. This ratio uses items found on the balance sheet such as cash, accounts receivable, inventory, accounts payable, and short-term debts.

Quick Ratio: The quick ratio is a slightly more aggressive version of the current ratio. This ratio is often referred to as an acid test ratio. While the current ratio includes all current assets, the quick ratio excludes certain current assets, such as inventory, in order to determine what would occur if a company has to repay its debts immediately. The quick ratio uses cash, cash equivalents, securities, and accounts receivable for its assets. The reason for using these assets is that they can be converted into cash very quickly. Unlike inventory, which must be sold before being converted into cash.

Cash Ratio: Honestly, this is just a more advanced version of the quick ratio. This ratio only uses cash and cash equivalents and compares them to all of its current liabilities. It excludes accounts receivables and securities.

Inventory Turnover: This ratio measures how long inventory remains in storage before it is sold. A low inventory turnover may indicate that a company has weak sales or bad marketing. On the other hand, an inventory turnover that is too fast may imply that a company has difficulty meeting the demand in the market. Regardless, investors find that this is a critical metric in determining the health of a company's sales.

Receivables Turnover: If inventory turnover is a measure of how well a company is doing at meeting current demand, receivables turnover is a measure of how well a company collects money that it is owed. For example, if a company allows its customers 90 days to pay for a product they purchased, the receivables turnover helps to show how much of that money was actually paid back to the company.

Working Capital Turnover: This ratio is used to see how efficiently a company is using its excess funds to promote sales. If this ratio is low, it indicates that a company is extremely inefficient at generating sales using its extra capital. Additionally, it may show that a company requires a large investment in marketing in order to generate new sales. This means that a company may require additional funds in order to become more efficient and sell more of their product.

Cash Conversion Cycle: This is a ratio that is extremely useful, and it can be used to show which companies are the most efficient in an industry. This formula relies on information such as how many days inventory, sales, and payables are outstanding. This ratio is also best used by upper management that are analyzing how well their firm is performing. This ratio is used over long periods of time to properly track a company's performance. This ratio shows how long it takes a company's investment in inventory and marketing to be converted into more money. It tracks how much time each dollar spends in production before turning into more dollars.

Solvency Ratios

The liquidity ratios above were used to analyze how well a company could pay off their short-term liabilities if the need arose. Solvency ratios are focused on long-term debts and a company's ability to pay those debts. These ratios are also called leverage ratios. If a company is over-levered, they risk bankruptcy and failure.

Total D/A: This is the total debt to total assets ratio. This ratio is used to determine how many assets a company owns in proportion to the total amount of debt that it has incurred. The higher this ratio, the more debt that a company has in comparison to its assets. The larger this ratio becomes, the riskier the company becomes as an investment and the more likely the company will fail to pay back its loans.

Total D/E: This is the total debt to total equity ratio. This ratio is used to determine how much equity a company's stockholders have in relation to a company's debt. With this ratio, investors are able to draw conclusions about a company's financial health. In the event of a decrease in business, this ratio can help show how much of the company's debt could be paid using shareholder equity. Similar to the D/A ratio, the higher this ratio is, the riskier the company.

Time Interest Earned: While many of these ratios require looking at a company's assets in proportion to its debt, this ratio focuses on the current income that a company has. With the TIE ratio, investors can see how well a company can pay its debt based on its current level of income. Effectively showing how much a company is chained to its debts. This ratio is great for determining the overall riskiness of a corporation in its current state.

All financial ratio calculations

Valuation Ratios	
EPS	$\frac{\text{Net income – Preferred Dividends}}{\text{Weighted average of Common shares Outstanding}}$
P/E Ratio	$\frac{\text{Current Stock Price}}{\text{EPS}}$
PEG Ratio	$\frac{\text{P/E ratio}}{\text{EPS * growth rate}}$
P/B Ratio	$\frac{\text{Current Stock Price}}{\text{Book value per share}}$
P/S Ratio	$\frac{\text{Current Stock Price}}{\text{Sales per share}}$

Profitability Ratios	
Gross Margin	Net Sales – Cost of Goods Sold
Operating Margin	$\frac{\text{EBIT}}{\text{Revenue}}$
Net Profit Margin	$\frac{\text{Net Income}}{\text{Revenue.}}$ *100
ROE	$\frac{\text{Net Income}}{\text{Shareholder's Equity}}$
ROA	$\frac{\text{Net Income}}{\text{Total Assets}}$
ROI	$\frac{\text{Current Value of Investment – Initial Cost of Investment}}{\text{Initial Cost of Investment}}$

Liquidity Ratios	
Current Ratio	$\frac{\text{Current Assets}}{\text{Current Liabilities}}$
Quick Ratio	$\frac{\text{Cash + Cash Equivalents + Securities + Accounts Receivable}}{\text{Current Liabilities}}$
Cash Ratio	$\frac{\text{Cash + Cash Equivalents}}{\text{Current Liabilities}}$
Inventory Turnover	$\frac{\text{Cost of Goods Sold}}{\text{Average Inventory}}$
Receivables Turnover	$\frac{\text{Net Sales made on credit}}{\text{Average Account Receivables}}$
Working Capital Turnover	$\frac{\text{Net Sales}}{\text{Average Working Capital}}$
CCC	DIO + DSO - DPO
DIO Days Inventory Outstanding	$\frac{\text{Average inventory}}{\text{Cost of Goods Sold}}$ *365
DSO Days Sales Outstanding	$\frac{\text{Average Accounts Receivable}}{\text{Revenue per day}}$
DPO Days Payable Outstanding	$\frac{\text{Average Accounts Payable}}{\text{Cost of Goods Sold/365}}$

Solvency Ratios	
Total D/A	$\frac{\text{Total Debt}}{\text{Total Assets}}$
Total D/E	$\frac{\text{Total Debt}}{\text{Shareholder's Equity}}$
TIE Times Interest Earned	$\frac{\text{EBITDA}}{\text{Interest Expense}}$

3.

Bond Market

Ah yes, the bond market. Maybe at some point in your life someone bought a bond for you. Probably a Great-Grandfather who wanted to be funny or thought that it would be worth more in the future. It's a cute moment or a nice gesture and then everyone forgets about it and moves on. After all, who cares about a bunch of papers that say that someone somewhere owes you money? In reality, bonds are the backbone of a company's capital and are used to finance projects all across the world in every industry. They are actually more valuable than many realize.

To start, we need to know exactly what a bond is. While a stock represented ownership in a company, a bond is a **debt** that the company must pay back. Whoever is the holder of the debt is referred to as the bondholder or debtholder. Like most loans, they must be paid back with interest. On a bond, the interest rate and interest payments are referred to as the coupon rate and coupon payments. At the end of the term, the bond pays back the principle amount. Bonds are a popular investment among individuals looking for income over time. The reason being that regular coupon payments are made to bondholders that grant a source of income.

The bond market shares many similarities with the stock market in the way that it operates. When a company wants to issue a bond to the public, they announce a new bond issue. The company then sets a price for the bond and sell it on the open market. After the bond has been issued, it continues to be bought and sold by investors on the open market. Ultimately, the market continues to operate as long as companies have capital needs to meet. Instead of dealing directly with a bank, the company decides to obtain a loan from the public in the form of bonds.

Before we delve too deeply into the world of bonds, this book will be referencing several different terms that are commonplace among bond investors. Specifically, these are terms that are common on any bond, and they are the first things that investors focus on when making a bond purchasing decision.

Par value: This is the principle amount of the bond at maturity. This is the amount that will be paid back to the bondholder at the end of the bond's term. Do not confuse par value with a bond's price. A bond may be trading at a price lower or higher than what the par value is.

Maturity: A bond's maturity is how much time is remaining on the bond before the par value needs to be paid back. If a bond has a remaining maturity of 5 years, then the bond's par value will be paid back in 5 years.

Coupon Rate: The coupon rate is the interest that is being paid on the bond over the lifetime of the bond. If a bond has a coupon rate of 7%, then the bondholder will receive 7% of the bond's par value in a year.

Example: par value = $1,000.

Coupon rate = 7%

Interest paid in a year: $70

Coupon Payment: The coupon payment can be derived from the coupon rate above. The reason why these are two distinct terms is because many bonds pay out on an annual, semi-annual, or quarterly basis. If the interest to be paid in a year is $70, then each coupon payment will be whatever payment schedule the bond is set for. If the coupon payment is set on a quarterly basis then the coupon payment is $70/4 = $17.50

Discount vs Premium: In the bond market, a bond is typically referred to as trading at a premium or discount. This has everything to do with what the price of the bond is in relation to the par value. Assume a bond's par value is $1,000. If a bond is being sold for $1,120, it is being sold at a premium. Conversely, if a bond is being sold for $986 then it is being sold at a discount. The reason why a bond may be trading lower than its par value will be explained later on in this chapter. For now, understand the difference between a bond being sold at a premium versus a discount.

Who Issues Bonds?

Bonds are issued by entities all throughout the world. While every bond issue is unique, we can classify bonds based on the entity that is issuing them. **Bonds can be issued by governments, agencies, and corporations.**

If a bond is issued by a country's government, investors have different ways to refer to the bonds based on the issuing country. For example, bonds issued by the United States are referred to as Treasury bonds. A Japanese bond would be referred to as a Japanese government bond. In Germany, a government bond is referred to as a bund. Basically, investors have a special way to refer to any country's bonds. For this book, we will be focusing on Treasury bonds.

Some people may avoid a country's bond and instead invest in a specific province of that country instead. Most countries, however, do not allow their provinces to issue their own bonds. The

United States is quite unique in this regard as the individual states themselves can also issue their own bonds. These bonds are referred to as municipal bonds or munis for short. Municipal bonds often get special attention because many of them offer tax advantages to those that purchase them.

Similar to municipal bonds, Federal agencies can also issue their own bonds. These are referred to as agency bonds. Do you have a lot of student loan debt? Sallie Mae, one of the largest lenders of student loans, actually bundles your debt together and sells it to investors. Agency bonds may or may not be backed by the U.S. government.

Lastly, bonds are also issued by corporations. These bonds are the most important as they are the main asset that investors are looking at buying. Corporate bonds are the riskiest bond to invest in, but they also have the highest yields. When looking at buying a corporate bond, investors want to know how likely a company is to default on the bond payment. Bonds are worthless if the bond issuer fails to pay on time.

What Affects a Bond's Price?

If we start to analyze and watch bonds, we start to realize several things. For one, the prices of similar bonds are completely different. Additionally, bonds often have special provisions that allow the bondholder or company to take an action that would affect the bond in some way. As a result, we need to understand the factors that go into the bond market and affect the price of individual bonds.

The biggest factor in the bond market is the current **market interest rate**. This is the current rate that a bond's coupon rate is being issued. The best way to explain this is to use two bonds that are issued from the same company. For this example, we are assuming that the company has remained stable over the course of a year and that the only thing that has changed in a year is the market interest rate.

Assume an investor purchases a bond for $1,000 at an interest rate of 4%, and they have held the bond for a year. After the year ends, the same company that they purchased a bond from is issuing another bond for $1,000 at an interest rate of 7%. Because a new bond is being issued at a higher interest rate, the price of the bond the investor initially purchased will decrease because a new bond is being issued at a higher interest rate. If the investor who bought a bond at 4% attempts to sell the bond on the market, they will find that people are not willing to pay $1,000 for a bond with a lower interest rate than the overall market. So, **if market interest rates rise then it decreases the price of issued bonds, but if market interest rates fall then it increases the value of existing bonds.**

What about inflation? Inflation can also decrease the price of bonds over time as well. After all, if inflation increases year after year, then bondholders may find that the return on their bonds may fail to keep up with inflation. If this occurs, then the coupon rate required of investors will also increase as investors may feel that they require a higher return on their investment to keep up with rising inflation.

Lastly, credit risk also greatly affects a stock's price. Bonds are typically rated by third-party rating agencies. Rating agencies like Standard and Poor's, Fitch, and Moody rank bonds based on their riskiness to an investor. If a bond has a higher risk of defaulting on a loan, it is rated lower by these agencies. If a bond's rating becomes too low, investors refer to those bonds as "junk bonds." If a company appears to be preparing for bankruptcy, then the bond price will drop in response. It should be noted that a lower rated bond will have to issue a higher interest rate and lower the purchasing price in order to convince investors to purchase the bond. A bond's price will also drop if one of these agencies decides to drop the bond's rating suddenly in the middle of the bond's lifetime. These are the factors that influence a bond's price, but what about a bond's coupon rate?

What Affects a Bond's Coupon Rate?

Now that we understand the outside factors that can affect a bond's market price, we can discuss the factors that affect a bond's interest rate. Here, we have a wonderful little formula that is taught across universities all throughout the Unites States. Seriously, ask any half-way decent finance student and they can quote this formula by heart. This formula helps us by walking through all of the risks that are associated with bonds.

$$R = R^* + IP + DRP + MRP + LP$$

Yes, I know what you're thinking. Is it seriously just addition? Unfortunately, Finance students aren't known for our outstanding mental prowess. Asking us to find what a bond's rate should be is easy, but don't expect us to understand something complicated like the complexities of quantum entanglement theory. Anyway, here is what all those symbols above stand for.

R: Interest rate. This is what the interest rate of the bond should be after taking into account the following factors.

R*: This is known as the risk-free interest rate. This number is considered to be theoretical in nature. It is the interest rate that an investor would require on an investment that could not fail. Where, however, can an investor find a risk-free asset? Investors often use the 3-month Treasury bond that the United States issues as the risk-free rate. The logic behind this decision is that the United States cannot fail to pay their debts. After all, they can simply print the money and give it to investors if they are unable to pay their debts. Additionally, the 3-month bond has a short term and provides investors with a good snapshot of the current rates.

IP: Inflation premium is the extra interest that investors ask for to keep up with rising inflation. If inflation is rising rapidly, investors will require a higher rate to keep up with their dollars losing purchasing power over time.

DRP: This part of the formula is the default risk premium. This is the extra interest rate that investors require from riskier bonds. If company A is more likely than company B to default on their bonds, then company A will have to issue their bonds at a higher interest rate in order to convince investors to take the risk. This is a double-edged sword, however, because company A is a riskier corporation, but they will have higher payments than company B to keep up with the bonds that they issued. Additionally, safer companies can issue bonds with lower interest rates than their riskier counterparts.

MRP: This is the maturity risk premium. Usually, the longer the bond term, the higher the interest rate. The reason being that the bond may run into issues later on, and investors want to be paid a higher interest rate for bearing that risk. Because of this higher risk, investors expect to be paid more.

LP: The liquidity premium is the premium that investors require of investments that are difficult to convert into cash. Certain bonds are difficult to sell and may not find a buyer easily. Because of this, some bonds may need to pay a higher amount in order to compensate for the illiquidity of the asset.

So, after hearing all of this you may be wondering how these premiums are calculated in order to get the right interest rate to issue a bond. Get ready to get your heart broken. The reality is that a lot of this information is theoretical in nature. Additionally, these premiums are usually **estimated** by the people that are issuing them. They learn whether they underestimated or overestimated based on how the market responds to their bond issuance. Regardless, this formula is an important tool to understand what goes through an investor's mind when they are considering purchasing bonds.

Two Types of Bonds: Secured vs Unsecured

In general, investors need to understand that there are typically two types of bonds that are listed on the market. While bonds can be categorized based on the issuer, bonds are also separated into two distinct classes. Those classes are secured and unsecured.

A secured bond has an asset attached to the bond. The asset can be a property, equipment, or income stream. The asset is used as collateral in the event that the issuer fails to pay the bondholder. If this occurs, the bondholder has a claim to the asset on the bond and can do whatever they want with the asset.

For example, say that a bond has a semi-truck listed as collateral in the event that the issuer fails to pay the bondholder. If the issuer fails to pay, the bondholder has a legal claim to the truck. They can then sell the truck and attempt to recuperate some of their losses.

An extremely common secured bond is a mortgage-backed security. These bonds are usually secured by the physical asset of the borrower and the income stream that comes from the mortgage payments. While this extra security is appreciated, bondholders are usually not able to cover all of their losses when a bond fails.

The other class of bonds is unsecured bonds. These types of bonds are also referred to as debentures. This type of bond is more common than secured bonds. These bonds are not collateralized by an asset. Instead, they are backed by the "full faith and credit" of the issuer. The issuer is effectively putting their reputation on the line to pay the bonds on a regular basis.

A bond being secured or unsecured can often affect the coupon rate on the bond. Assume two bonds are issued by the same company, one is secured and the other is unsecured. The bond that is secured should have the lower coupon rate because some of the risk has been collateralized by an asset. The unsecured asset has to make up for not being safer by offering a higher interest rate to investors.

Situations can arise where an unsecured bond actually has a lower interest rate than a secured bond. This occurs when two different companies are issuing a bond. This typically occurs because the firm issuing the unsecured bond is considered to be extremely safe and carries very little risk. Even if a bond is secured by an asset, a company that seems like it may declare bankruptcy at any minute will have to offer an extremely high interest rate for their bonds in order to attract any investors.

Types of Bonds

Now that we understand the difference between secured bonds and debentures, we can focus on the more specific types of bonds that are issued. These bonds can either be secured or unsecured. The differences between these bonds has to do with interest rates, issuing currency, and risk level.

Fixed Rate Bonds: All of the examples used up until this point are fixed rate bonds. A fixed rate bond has a set coupon rate that is established when the bond is issued. The coupon rate does not change and will remain the same until the bond reaches its maturity.

Floating Rate Bonds: A floating rate bond is a bond that has a coupon rate that changes throughout the bond's lifetime. A floating rate bond is typically attached to a rate that a third-party issued. Many bonds are based off of the federal funds rate or the London Interbank Offered Rate (LIBOR). For example, a bond may be quoted at a price of LIBOR + 3.2%. If the current LIBOR is 2.3%, then the bond coupon rate would be 5.5%. The bond's coupon rate would then change throughout the life of the bond based on whether the LIBOR rate increased or decreased. These bonds are great for reducing interest rate risk, but the coupon payments can vary throughout the life of the bond. If market rates rise, then the investor does not care because his bond payments will increase. If it falls, then the investor will witness a decrease in their regular payments. Using these bonds will remove some of the volatility of changing bond prices, but also the potential profit to be made from selling fixed rate bonds when market rates drop.

Zero Coupon Bonds: A zero coupon bond is a bond that does not pay investors at regular intervals. These bonds are sold at steep discounts to the par value. After the bond matures, the investor receives the par value all at once. For example, a zero-coupon bond may be sold for $550 with a par value of $1,000. If we assume a one-year maturity, then an investor will pay $550 up front and receive $1,000 in a year. During the one-year maturity period, investors will not receive any payments. It should be noted, that these bonds can be risky for two reasons. The first is default risk. If the bond issuer defaults on the bond, then the investor will receive no money. Additionally, interest rates may rise suddenly and force the zero bonds to be worth less than they would have initially. A similar danger occurs when you consider inflation as a factor that erodes at the value of the money that the investor receives at the bond's maturity.

Eurobonds: A Eurobond is a bond that is issued in another country's currency. People often become confused with Eurobonds because they think that a Eurobond is a bond that is issued in a European country or in Euros. That is not the case. In reality, a Eurobond refers to any bond that is issued in another currency that is not the home country's currency. For example, a Chinese company could issue a bond in U.S. dollars. That bond would be referred to as a Eurobond. Eurobonds have become extremely popular in recent years in emerging markets. Emerging markets use Eurobonds because their own currencies may be extremely volatile and difficult to predict. As a result, emerging markets can attract investors by issuing bonds in a safer and more stable currency.

International Bonds: An international bond is a bond that is issued by a foreign entity to the investor. They can also be classified as any of the bonds that we have described above. Typically, a foreign entity will issue these bonds in the investor's domestic market.

Grading Bonds

If you have ever gone to school, you have likely received a grade at some point in your life. Similar to receiving a good or bad grade on your report card, bonds are also graded. As mentioned earlier, bonds are graded by third-party agencies that determine how risky a bond is. Some of the well-known grading agencies are Moody's, Standard and Poor's, and Fitch. The companies have similar grading scales, and investors use those ratings to evaluate how safe an investment might be. Professional portfolio managers also use these ratings to determine how much of their portfolios they want allocated to each investment grade. The grading scale for these companies ranges from AAA/Aaa to C/D.

When classifying these bonds, investors refer to bonds as either being investment grade or junk bonds. An investment grade bond usually has a rating of BBB/Baa or higher. Junk bonds are rated at BB/Ba or lower. Additionally, junk bonds are referred to as "fallen angels" and "rising stars." A fallen angel is a bond that was once considered to be investment grade, but they have now fallen into a junk bond rating because the company has become unreliable. On the other hand, a rising star is a company that has had their rating increased. These bonds might still be considered junk bonds, but the company's reliability seems to be moving in the right direction.

Each rating that a bond receives is a reflection of the safety of that bond. As the rating goes lower, the bond's risk increases and quality decreases. As a result, companies want to be ranked as highly as possible. The safer a company is, the lower the coupon rate they can place on their bonds. After all, it is easier to attract investors if you have a reliable and secure company that doesn't default on their loans. Below is a comparison chart for the different bond rating agencies, the different ratings that they assign to bonds, and what each rating represents.

Bond Rating			[redacted]	
Moody's	**S&P**	**Fitch**	Grade	Rating Definition
Aaa	AAA	AAA	Investment	Highest quality, lowest risk
Aa1	AA+	AA+	Investment	High quality, low risk
Aa2	AA	AA	Investment	High quality, low risk
Aa3	AA-	AA-	Investment	High quality, low risk
A1	A+	A+	Investment	Upper medium quality, low risk
A2	A	A	Investment	Upper medium quality, low risk
A3	A-	A-	Investment	Upper medium quality, low risk
Baa1	BBB+	BBB+	Investment	Medium quality, medium risk
Baa2	BBB	BBB	Investment	Medium quality, medium risk
Baa3	BBB-	BBB-	Investment	Medium quality, medium risk
Ba1	BB+	BB+	Junk	Speculative, high risk
Ba2	BB	BB	Junk	Speculative, high risk
Ba3	BB-	BB-	Junk	Speculative, high risk
B1	B+	B+	Junk	Low quality, High risk
B2	B	B	Junk	Low quality, High risk
B3	B-	B-	Junk	Low quality, High risk
Caa1	CCC+	CCC	Junk	Low quality, Highest risk
Caa2	CCC	CC	Junk	Low quality, Highest risk
Caa3	CCC-	C	Junk	Low Quality, highest risk
Ca	CC	DDD	Junk	Low quality, highest risk
C	C	DD	Junk	May be in default
D	D		Junk	In default

Special Bond Characteristics

Every bond is special and unique because every issuing entity is special and unique. Some bonds, however, have special terms that change the way that the bonds function. Here is a list of special bond characteristics that can influence the price investors are willing to pay for a bond. This is not a list of every single special bond, but it covers the most common ones.

Callable bonds: A callable bond is a special feature that some bonds have. If a bond is callable, it means that the issuing entity can choose to recall the bond at a specific price and time. If the bond is recalled, it is recalled at a call premium. The call premium is usually higher than the par value for the bond. This means that the issuer would have to pay more to recall those bonds from investors. If the bond is recalled, investors receive the premium and have to look for a new investment opportunity. This begs the question, however, why would a company want to pay more to recall bonds from investors? Ultimately, it has everything to do with the market interest rates when the bond was issued versus the current market rates. Callable bonds are typically enacted when the bond was issued during a period of high market interest rates. Eventually, the market interest rates may fall. If the rates fall far enough, it is beneficial for the company to call the bonds they had issued and re-issue the bonds under the lower interest rate. As a result, bonds are typically called if interest rates have fallen to a point where it is more beneficial to re-pay the bonds and the call premium in order to have lower interest payments. Typically, callable bonds have a higher coupon rate as investors bear the risk of having to reinvest their money at a lower rate in the future.

Puttable bonds: A puttable bond is the opposite of a callable bond. A puttable bond gives the bondholder the right to return the bond back to the issuer at a specified time and date. The bondholder has the right to receive the principal amount at an earlier time than specified on the bond. Because this is a feature that benefits bondholders, the issuer can issue these bonds at a lower interest rate. In addition to the lower coupon rate, investors will often pay a premium to obtain these bonds because of the added flexibility. Why would an investor want to force a company to pay back a bond at an earlier date? In the case of a puttable bond, an investor would force the issuer to pay back the bond if interest rates have risen. With a puttable bond, investors can mitigate some of their reinvestment risk. If market interest rates are higher at the time when investors can regain the money on their bonds, they can turn around and reinvest that money at the new higher market rate.

Convertible Bonds: While the previous two bonds were special because they changed the maturity date of the bonds, this bond is special because it changes the underlying asset entirely. A convertible bond changes the debt obligation into a portion of ownership in the company. The bond converts from a debt to company stock at a pre-set price. Investors can use these bonds to cash in on companies that have had sudden increases in their stock price.

Income Bonds: Income bonds also cash in on the increasing value of a company. An income bond only pays a coupon payment if the issuing entity makes a profit. In simple terms, an investor purchases an income bond. The bond does not have a set coupon payment because it goes up and down depending on how much profit the company is generating. At the end of the bond's maturity, the investor receives the par value of the investment.

Step-up/Step-down bonds: This type of bond has coupon payments that either increase or decrease over the maturity of the bond. Typically, companies that are expecting an increase or decrease in revenue will issue these bonds. These bonds are less popular, but they are seen occasionally. The coupon rate changes are set in advance and the bond follows the predetermined payment schedule.

While there are other bonds that are issued on a regular basis, they tend to be uncommon and often confuse people learning about the bond market. If there is one thing in this section that is important, it is callable bonds. Companies love to issue callable bonds because it gives them control over interest rates when they fall. Additionally, it can allow the company to lower their interest payments by forcing investors to buy their new bonds at the lower rate or go elsewhere. This provision is common and can hurt investors if they are not careful.

Bond Valuations

this section covers what investors may calculate when determining whether to purchase a bond or not. If you don't care, then skip to the next chapter

So, remember that formula that we saw in the beginning that was all about understanding what goes into a bond's interest rate. Unfortunately, most of that is theoretical in nature. It serves as a great teaching tool to show the potential risks associated with bonds, but in reality, investors use the interest rates that they get from different bonds and calculate how profitable each bond is.

In essence, investors obtain the information that they need on the market and then use different formulas to compare the bonds to each other. By having set formulas, they can evaluate bonds on a number of different criteria and determine how to proceed. Such formulas include current yield, yield to maturity, yield to call, and expected future cash flows.

In theory, a bond's price should always be reflected in its future cash flows, but we all know that outside factors can cause a bond's price to drop drastically. Knowing that, we will assume that outside conditions remain the same throughout the life of a bond.

The most basic way to price a bond is to look at the present value of a bond's future cash flows. The future value versus the present value is an important aspect of any investment. Due to inflation, the value of a dollar today will not be worth the same 20 years from now. That is why investors discount the future coupon payments they will receive in order to account for inflation. The formula used for general bond pricing is on the next page.

Bond Price = $\sum_{i=1}^{n} C/(1+r)^n + F/(1+r)^N$

C = Coupon Payment

r = Yield to Maturity (YTM)

F = Bond's Par Value

n = Time

N = Number of Periods until the Bond's Maturity Date

This formula has two main components. The first component is the regular coupon payments that the investor receives. The second component is the final payment that is received when the bond matures. Here is an example bond to show how the formula is applied.

Par value: $1,000

Coupon rate: 5%

Coupon payments: $50

Payment schedule: annual

Maturity: 5 years

Yield to Maturity (YTM): 7%

Then we use these numbers and the formula to obtain the following result.

$P = 50/(1.07)^1 + 50/(1.07)^2 + 50/(1.07)^3 + 50/(1.07)^4 + 1{,}050/(1.07)^5$

$P = 46.73 + 43.67 + 40.82 + 38.15 + 748.64$

$P = \$918.01$

Using the formula, we are able to see what the bond should be worth at its current interest rate. In this formula, the YTM represents the market interest rates. If the market interest rate were to decrease, it would increase the price of the bond. If the YTM was equal to the coupon rate, then the bond should be priced at its par value. This formula allows us to see the inverse relationship between market interest rates and a bond's coupon rate.

If $r >$ coupon rate, then $P <$ par value

If $r =$ coupon rate, then $P =$ par value

If $r <$ coupon rate, then $P >$ par value

This formula is often adjusted for different bonds that have different payment schedules. For example, some bonds pay out semi-annually or quarterly. In those cases, you divide the coupon payment by the number of periods in a year, and you divide the YTM by the number of periods in a year. From there, you have to calculate each and every payment until you arrive to the final payment. The formula can be adjusted, but it can be tedious to manually make those adjustments.

The next step in understanding bond valuations are the various methods investors use to calculate the overall yield on a bond. The yield measures are used to show what the return on a bond will be on a percentage basis.

The first yield measure is the yield to maturity. You should remember the yield to maturity from the formula that we just covered. You should also remember that almost everything that is done with these formulas is purely hypothetical. That holds true for the yield to maturity as well.

When professional investors want to get a true yield to maturity, they will use trial and error to obtain a YTM that matches the overall market. They do this by viewing the current price that a bond is selling for, and then plugging in numbers into the above formula until a YTM appears that most accurately conforms to the current price the bond is selling at.

The other method to obtaining the YTM is the approximation method. In the real world, it is much easier for investors to obtain the price of a bond than the YTM. That is why this formula can be used to approximate the real YTM.

$$YTM = \frac{C + \frac{FV - PV}{T}}{\frac{FV + PV}{2}}$$

C = Coupon Payment

FV = Par Value

PV = Market Price

T = Years to Maturity

This formula gives investors a picture into what the YTM should approximately be. It should be noted that professionals typically use a calculator or Excel in order to obtain the YTM on a regular basis. Without a computer, they would waste significant time calculating each and every bond's YTM.

Lastly, we have the yield to call. Remember how some bonds can be called back early by a company if they want to. Well when calculating what a bond's yield to call is, we assume that the company will call the bond. If the bond is called early, it changes the yield that an investor will receive on the bond. Again, the formula is usually modified to fit the need of the call. In reality, a computer will give an investor the yield to call very quickly without all the extra algebra. Today, computers are used to calculate all of this, but if you wanted to know what the actual formulas were behind the computers, here they are.

4.

Money Market

The money market is not to be confused with the foreign exchange market. (Chapter 5) The money market refers to the buying and selling of short-term securities. These are basical y bonds with very short maturities. The maturities on these securities can range from one day to one year. The majority of securities in the money market have a maturity of three months or less.

Because the overall market has low maturities on their securities, the market is considered to be extremely liquid. So liquid, that some institutions will use them to transfer large amounts of funds at any given time. The money market is seldom thought of, but it is the backbone of the financial economy.

The money market is also considered to be extremely safe. While it has extremely low returns, its stability stands out. The goal of the money market is to never lose money. Effectively, the market should just perfectly keep up with inflation over long periods of time. Whatever currency is kept in the money market should perfectly retain its value when it is withdrawn. If $1 is placed in the money market, it should still be worth $1 when it is taken out in six months. It should not be worth $0.95 from when it was originally invested. The money market will not make anybody rich, but it will store the value of their currency until it needs to be withdrawn.

While individual investors can purchase money market mutual funds in order to have a place in the money market, individual investors are blocked from actually transacting in the market. The reality is that institutional investors are often the only people who can play in this market. Individuals often use this market as a way to park their money inflation free until they need it.

Institutional investors, however, use the money market for a variety of reasons. For example, a company may require cash immediately to avoid insolvency. Banks often fall into this category. If a bank needs funds to meet a large withdraw, they may borrow from the money market to obtain the liquidity they need. There are several categories of the money markets that are distinct. Each category can be considered to be a different type of security, and we will go over each of them.

Institutional investors also use the money market to meet short-term obligations when they arise. Typically, there is a disconnect between when an asset generates income and a liability requires payment. The money market is excellent at solving this problem because it allows for the smooth transfer of funds on a short-term basis for an institution to meet its obligations. Without the money market, institutions would have to be extremely cautious with their investments, and the financial economy would become very inefficient. After all, if an institution will not lend money to people who need it, the economy will slow down to adjust to the lack of funds flowing in and out.

It should be noted that while the securities sold on the money market may have a short maturity, the amounts being moved are by no means trivial. Transactions in the money market easily range between $5 million to over $1 billion per transaction. That is why this market is reserved for institutions and not individuals.

The money supply that flows into the market is provided by individual savers, corporations with extra money to move around, and the Federal Reserve. The demand for this capital is comprised of governments, banks, and corporations that need to meet regulatory requirements.

At the end of the day, the money market deals primarily with debt that matures in **less than a year.** It is immensely important to any financial economy and allows financial institutions to flow without facing a potential collapse.

Players in the Money Market

Before we look at the types of securities sold in the money market, we need to focus on the players in this market. After all, a game is nothing without its players.

Governments: Governments use the money markets to raise capital for when they need it. Specifically, the U.S. Treasury uses the money markets to raise funds by selling short-term obligations called Treasury Bills. Treasury Bills are considered to be free of default risk. Because of this, Treasury Bills often offer the lowest interest rates in the money market. Each country typically has their own money market. Some examples include the Canadian, Japanese, and German money markets. These governments also issue their own form of a Treasury Bill into the money market. A government is capable of greatly influencing the overall money market. They can do this by increasing or decreasing the interest rate offered on their Treasury Bills and other securities that they issue.

Banks: To a bank, the money market is one of the most important tools that they use to facilitate their transactions. To start, banks borrow from the money market to fund many of their business activities. With this extra capital, they can issue more loans with the funds received from individuals and continue to stay afloat. The money market is very important because banks are extremely regulated. Part of their regulations are that they must maintain a certain portion of their assets as cash. If a bank starts to fall below that requirement, they may borrow funds from the money market in order to meet those requirements. Also, did you know that banks borrow money from other banks? When a bank needs funds, they may borrow the funds from another bank. The bank charges interest for the duration of the loan until it is returned. These loans are very short-term. Sometimes the banks are simply borrowing money overnight and return it the next day. The interest that is charged when a bank borrows money from another bank is called the federal funds rate. **This is where people get confused.** The federal funds rate is not the interest that is charged when a bank borrows funds from the Federal Reserve. Make no mistake, they can do both in the money market, but the interest that is charged when a bank borrows from the Federal Reserve is referred to as the discount rate. Why is this an important distinction to even make? It's important for public policy. Have you ever watched the news and heard someone say that the Federal Reserve is planning to increase or decrease the federal funds rate? When the Federal Reserve announces that, they are referring to a target that they would like to hit. By raising or dropping the discount rate, the Fed can force banks to lower or decrease the rates that they charge each other. They cannot, however, actually change the rate that the banks charge each other to borrow funds. They only influence the rate by increasing and decreasing the discount rate. Typically, when the Federal Reserve wants to stimulate the economy, they drop the federal funds target rate. When they want to weaken the economy, they increase the target rate. While there are other things that the banks do in the money market, we can cover those later. For now, understand the role of the Federal Reserve in influencing and controlling the interest rates in the money markets.

Companies: Another player in the money markets are companies. If a company is playing in the money market, it is usually a large corporation that is extremely trustworthy. These companies use the money markets to raise funds. Think of it like a company issuing a bond, but individual investors cannot pick which ones to buy because only institutions get to play in the market. When a company attempts to raise funds in the money market, they issue commercial paper. Similar to everything in this market, commercial paper has a very short maturity. Institutions like commercial paper because it usually has a higher rate of return than anything else in the market. Naturally, companies are considered to be the riskiest investments. Especially when compared to the government and large institutional banks. Lastly, international companies use the money markets to ensure certain transactions will go through. They do this through banker's acceptances. These notes are insured by banks that offer a discount on the face value of the banker's acceptance. The bank then ensures the banker's acceptance by being required to honor the acceptance. International companies use these to finalize transactions with little to no risk between the two parties.

Dealers and Brokers: This is the first party in this list that does not issue securities in the money market. In a sense, dealers and brokers are closer to the stadium and fans versus actually playing in the money market. The money market depends on these entities to market and promote new securities when they are listed and to provide a secondary market where securities can be bought and sold before they mature. Dealers often act as intermediaries between participants in the money market. They help to provide a location where borrowers and lenders can meet. Effectively, they act as a stadium. Brokers will take a commission for matching buyers and sellers in the money market. In a sense, they are the fans that come to the stadium to watch the game. This is an oversimplification of the roles brokers and dealers play, but they do serve a unique and useful role in this market.

Federal Reserve: Wait, didn't we cover the Federal Reserve in the banks section? Yes, we did. Remember how the Federal Reserve was focused on maintaining a stable economy by manipulating the market interest rates? Well, these are the mechanisms for manipulating the money markets. The Federal Reserve has several roles in this market. The first is the control over the money supply. The Federal Reserve controls this through the purchasing and selling of Treasury Bills. In effect, the Federal Reserve actually has more control over the federal funds rate than the U.S. Treasury does. When the Federal Reserve purchases or sells Treasury Bills, it is referred to as open market operations. As covered before, they can also manipulate the rate by changing the discount rate that is offered to banks. The other role of the Federal Reserve in the market is being a "lender of last resort." When a bank is having immense financial difficulties, they may require a loan from the Federal Reserve. In this sense, the Federal Reserve ensures that a bank will not fail and take all of their clients' money with them. Institutions are always concerned with the actions the Federal Reserve will take as it can directly affect the decisions that they will make.

Individuals: Individuals cannot play in the money market. Instead, they have to band together to create their own player. This is accomplished through a money market mutual fund. These funds pool together individuals' money and use the money to purchase securities in the money market. They then issue shares to investors based on how much money each investor put in. This is currently the only way that individuals can gain access to the money market. Even then, they must go through a broker to do so.

Securities that are sold in the Money Market

Now that we understand who plays in the money market, we should also understand the types of securities that are being bought and sold. We already covered a couple of securities like commercial paper and Treasury bills. They are included below as well, but you should already have a basic understanding of these financial instruments.

Treasury Bills: Remember T-bills? They are issued by the U.S. Treasury. Naturally, these securities are backed by the U.S. Government. These securities can be purchased directly from the U.S. Treasury. They have four maturities: 30, 90, 180, and 360 days. These bills are issued as zero-coupon bonds. Meaning that they are issued at a discount to face value. The interest is represented by the difference between the face value and discounted purchase price.

Certificate of Deposit: A certificate of deposit (CD) is a certificate that is issued by a bank. Not all CD's are considered to be money market securities, but there are some CD's with short maturities between three to six months. A certificate of deposit has a set interest rate and will penalize the investor if they attempt to withdraw the money early. This security is a literal IOU from a bank. The interest rate is set at the beginning of the CD, and it will not change throughout its lifetime.

Commercial Paper: We already covered commercial paper pretty extensively, but here is an overview. It is issued by corporations, and like everything in the money market it has a short maturity. The SEC has set the maximum maturity on commercial paper to be 270 days. Only safe and secure corporations can issue commercial paper. Commercial paper usually has a higher rate of return than other securities in the money market.

Banker's Acceptance: This type of security is interesting, but it can confuse people. In effect, this is a document that guarantees that a bank will pay the face value of the security in the future. A bank will only do this with a company that it believes is trustworthy. When the maturity is hit, the bank pays out the face value to the specified party. As mentioned above, a banker's acceptance is often used for foreign trade to ensure that both parties don't get burned. Like everything in the money market, it is a short-term loan. Specifically, it is very similar to a check that is written for a future date. The bank then ensures that the check will clear when the receiving party goes to cash it.

Repurchase Agreement: A repurchase agreement are Treasury securities that are purchased with the agreement that they will be sold back at a higher price. These securities are extremely liquid. Maturities can range from 24 hours to a few months. These are also referred to as repos. The Federal Reserve often buys repos as a way to regulate the overall money supply. To purchase a repo, firms will usually go through a dealer.

Eurodollars: A Eurodollar is an interesting part of the money market. To start, Eurodollars are U.S. dollars that are located in another country. Some of those bank accounts that hold Eurodollars are very large and are also in foreign countries. Often times, money market funds, individuals, banks, and companies will place their money into these bank accounts because they pay higher interest rates than the accounts they can find domestically. It should be noted that Eurodollar bank accounts are not subject to Federal Reserve regulations.

Federal Funds: Federal funds also play a part in the money market, but it is a privilege reserved for banks. Banks have requirements for the amount of funds they need to keep in reserve. Failure to meet those requirements can lead to a bank being forced to shut down. If a bank begins to come close to or fails to meet the requirement, they can borrow money from the Fed. Naturally, the bank will return the money with interest.

Putting it all together

You should now understand the money market, the institutions involved, and the types of securities that are issued. Below you can find a graphic that shows the different securities in the money market and the people who borrow or issue that security.

Security	Issuer	Buyer
Treasury Bills	Government	Banks, Companies, Individuals, Dealers and Brokers
Certificate of Deposit	Banks	Individuals
Commercial Paper	Banks, Companies	Banks, Companies
Banker's Acceptance	Banks	Banks
Repurchase Agreement	Federal Reserve, Dealers and Brokers	Dealers and Brokers, Companies, Banks
Eurodollars	Foreign Banks	Banks, Companies, Individuals
Federal Funds	Federal Reserve	Banks

5.

Foreign Exchange Market

The Foreign Exchange Market is one of the most interesting financial systems in the world. To start, this market is the largest in the world. The market volume in this market is over $5 trillion each day. Naturally, this means that the market is open to anyone that wants to trade. When talking about the Foreign Exchange Market, investors often refer to it as "forex."

It can be easy to confuse the money market and the Forex market. So, we will draw a clear distinction here. While the money market is used for the transfer of funds between institutions in the form of short-term debt, the Forex market refers to the active trading of different currencies. In the Forex market, investors exchange one currency for another.

Forex trading is considered to be a very high-risk investment. Enhancing that risk is the fact that many investors trade using margin which can lead to a larger loss than the initial money that was put in the market. This also means that Forex has more scammers than any other market. If you think your car's extended warranty expiring is a ridiculous scam, get ready for Forex scammers. These people will often request for you to give them a set amount of money that they will invest on your behalf to make you rich. To make matters worse, Forex is an extremely unregulated market. Meaning the money can be moved quickly and once a scammer has enough money, they can take it all and disappear.

Aside from the delinquents that perpetuate the Forex market, this market has one very special feature. Forex trades can occur 24/7. It does this by spreading the trading across four major exchanges across the world. Those exchanges are London, New York, Sydney, and Tokyo. If you need to refer to a chart for when each exchange is open, check out Chapter 1 where we went over the times each market is open.

Naturally, the primary asset that is traded in the Foreign Exchange Market are currencies. For example, dollars are exchanged for euros, euros are exchanged for yen, or yen are exchanged for pounds. The value of these currencies fluctuates and changes over time. As a result, an investor can lose or make money depending on whether or not the currency they are holding has gone up or down in value in comparison to their home currency.

The exchange rate for a currency is how much one unit of a currency will trade for another currency. So, if the exchange rate for

1 dollar to yen is 105, it means that 1 dollar can be traded for 105 yen. On the other hand, the exchange rate from 1 yen to dollar would be 0.009524 (1/105). Both exchange rates convey the same message. Forex traders are able to profit based on whether or not the exchange rate increases or decreases.

When the exchange rate for a currency rises, it is referred to as strengthening. When currency A strengthens in comparison to currency B, it means that one unit of currency A can now purchase more units of currency B then it previously could. When the exchange rate for a currency falls, it is referred to as weakening. When a currency weakens in comparison to another currency, the inverse effect occurs. Meaning that the weakened currency can now purchase less units of the other currency than before.

Overall, the entire forex market is controlled by the supply and demand for different currencies throughout the globe. First, we should explore the supply side of a currency. Supply of a currency is controlled by a central bank. Typically, that country's government gives orders to the central bank about how many bills to put into circulation.

On the other side of the equation, you have demand. Demand is controlled by commercial banks, foreign investors, and individuals. The more useable and stable a currency is, the more attractive they appear to investors looking to store their wealth. Similar to most products and commodities, the higher the demand for a currency climbs, the more valuable that currency becomes. If an oversupply of the currency occurs, people may view that as excessive inflation, and the currency may be avoided.

Okay, but why in the world should I care? After all, I don't travel anywhere, and I live in one country. So why should I care if my currency fluctuates in price in comparison to another country? That's a good point, so here is a great answer. Most likely you have purchased a good at some point in your life that was produced in a foreign country. This is important because it affects the relative price of domestic and foreign goods.

Here's an example, let's pretend that you are a wine snob. Also, we are assuming that you are an American with an extensive wine collection. To add to your collection, you would like to purchase a 1962 Chateau Mouton Rothschild. In order to obtain your wine, you must import it from France. Say the price of the wine is 750 euros and the current exchange rate is $1.23/euro. In this case, it would cost you $922.50 in order to get your wine. Perhaps, you decide that this is too high, and instead decide to wait a few months before making your purchase. Say six months later, the exchange rate is $1.52/euro. Now, it will cost you $1,140 to purchase your wine. That is a 23.58% increase. Naturally, you will be frustrated at being unable to add to your collection and may wait for the exchange rate to drop.

Okay, thank you for the example, but I don't import anything. I buy everything inside my country. Why should I care? You should care because exchange rates affect people purchasing items within their own countries the most. What, don't believe me? Alright, have you ever gone shopping and realized that many of the things you were purchasing were not manufactured inside your own country? There is a reason for that, and it has a lot to do with exchange rates. In the United States, this occurred in the mid-1980s.

During this time period, American businesses became less competitive than foreign corporations. This competitive disadvantage was attributed to the strengthening dollar. As the dollar became worth more, it made the price of American goods more expensive for foreigners. As a result, foreign countries did not want to purchase more expensive American products because the value of the dollar kept rising. Eventually, the dollar fell in value, but the effects have been seen ever since. Now, multi-national American companies produce goods in markets where the dollar is worth significantly more and sell the goods in the domestic American market or markets where the dollar is worth much less. With this, companies are able to make significantly more than if they were to produce goods inside of the United States.

This helps to explain why exchange rates are so important to a global and domestic economy, but it does not explain why currencies rise and fall in value in comparison to each other. To understand the markets, economists have developed several ways to explain the differing exchange rates between countries. While these theories are decent for the long run, they are horrible at predicting short-term changes. This is unfortunate because short-term changes are what most people in the forex market are concerned about.

Exchange Rate Theories

There are two major exchange rate theories for understanding the changes in exchange rates over a long period of time. Again, these theories are the absolute worst in the short-term. They are good for explaining exchange rates over long periods of time.

Law of One Price: This theory states that if two countries produce an identical good then the price of the good should be the same throughout the world no matter what country is producing it. This assumes that transportation costs are the same and that trade barriers are low. Additionally, it assumes that exchange rates would have to be equal to each other. If this theory were true, then arbitrage would be impossible. Arbitrage occurs when someone buys a good in one market and sells it in another market for a profit. Additionally, there are several barriers that make it almost impossible to observe the law of one price in the short term.

Several barriers include transportation costs, transaction costs, legal restrictions, and trade barriers.

Purchasing Power Parity (PPP): This theory is an extension of the Law of One Price. Purchasing Power Parity states that exchange rates between two currencies will adjust inversely to each other. It reflects those changes based on price increases among goods between two countries. **PPP states that if one country's price level rises in comparison to another country, its currency should depreciate while the other country's currency should appreciate.** For an example, let's assume that there is a 10% increase in the price level that Americans have to pay for their yearly expenses. PPP states that the Euro should appreciate by 10% against the dollar. Again, this theory has been helpful in predicting exchange rate changes over long periods of time, but it's terrible in the short-term.

Poking holes in Purchasing Power Parity (PPP)

By this point you may be reading about PPP and thinking to yourself that this is a baseless theory that clearly has not observed the real world. Honestly, you would be right. While the theory may work in the long-term, it is a terrible short-term indicator of how exchange rates will move. Here are some problems with the theory so we can move on from this boring topic.

Naturally, the most obvious problem with this theory is that it requires that two countries have almost identical transportation costs and trade restrictions. With immense confidence, we can assume that there are no countries that will have the exact same transportation costs alone. This is not even broaching the subject of the absolute maze of trade restrictions that countries have on various goods. To get around this problem, economists simply assume that there are no transportation costs or trade barriers. Hopefully, you are noticing a pattern of assuming anything that would take too much time to explain.

Regardless, another problem with the theory is that it cannot be applied to all produced goods. While it may be possible to compare goods like steel, it becomes extremely difficult to use this theory when goods become more complicated. In the consumer's mind, there is a large difference between a Mercedes-Benz and a Honda. While they may both be vehicles, purchasing power parity will be unable to explain the price differences between them.

Of course, this problem was eventually put to the test. In order to test PPP, The Economist, a newspaper, decided to test the theory using McDonalds. Specifically, the popular menu item known as the Big Mac. This newspaper started tracking the price of a Big Mac in

1986 and has not stopped yet. The Big Mac Index tracks the price of a Big Mac across different countries to test PPP.

In a shocking turn of events, PPP does not actually hold up. While part of the problem lies with the above issues, there are two other major issues with this theory. One is the non-tradable costs associated with a different location. These costs include utilities, labor, and overhead. These costs can even be viewed on a domestic scale. For example, a Big Mac might cost more in a city where rent is higher than in a small suburb.

The second problem with PPP is the assumption of perfect information. Purchasing Power Parity assumes that all individuals have perfect information about the prices of goods in other markets. While the internet has helped tremendously with being able to compare prices, individuals have far from perfect information on an international scale.

After absolutely trashing PPP, it should be noted that there is an updated version of this theory. While it still has some of the same flaws as PPP, it attempts to reconcile those issues. This new theory is called the "relative PPP theory." This new theory attempts to explain the continual inflation that countries experience. While this added benefit is nice, it still fails to explain many of the other issues discussed.

Factors that Affect Exchange Rates

All of these factors will affect exchange rates in the long run. While the forex market will eventually adjust to the new price level, it will not happen immediately. Fluctuations in price are not uncommon to observe during the short-term.

Relative Price Levels: This factor is the basis of the PPP theory. **When prices in one country go up, it depreciates that country's currency, and other countries' currencies will appreciate.** Of course, the inverse affect will occur if a country's price level decreases.

Inflation: Inflation is a huge factor when analyzing the way that a country's currency changes. **Countries with lower rates of inflation in comparison to other countries will see their currencies appreciate.** Inflation occurs when the prices of goods and services rise over time. The phrase "a dollar today is not a dollar tomorrow" illustrates the effect of inflation. If inflation rises too quickly, it is referred to as "hyperinflation" Countries that experience this often see the value of their currencies drop dramatically and find it difficult to retain foreign investors that are receiving compensation in a hyperinflated currency.

Interest rates: A country's interest rates are a major factor in influencing the exchange rate of a currency. **Increases in the interest rates cause a country's currency to appreciate.** The reverse is also true. This is due to the fact that lenders are rewarded as interest rates increase. As interest rates increase, it attracts foreign investors to that country's economy. As a result, it leads to an increased demand for that currency. Which leads to the currency appreciating over time.

Trade Barriers: Often times, countries erect trade barriers to protect domestic industries. This is generally accomplished through tariffs and quotas. A tariff is a tax on an imported good and a quota is a limit on the quantity of goods that can be imported. **When a trade barrier is erected, it tends to cause the country's currency to appreciate.** This is because domestic industries become more competitive than their foreign counterparts. As demand for domestic products increases, the currency will appreciate.

Consumer Preferences: "The customer is always right." This simple rule applies even to exchange rates. As consumers' preferences change, they can influence the exchange rate in the long run. An example would be American citizens developing an appetite for French wines and Japanese automobiles. Other countries may also develop new tastes. For example, German citizens wanting to taste

Florida Oranges and Chinese citizens wanting to watch American movies. **In effect, when demand increases for a country's exports it causes its currency to appreciate. If demand for imports increases within a country, it causes the domestic currency to depreciate.** The inverse also holds true if demand for exports decreases in foreign markets, and if demand for imports decreases.

Political Stability: The overall stability of a country plays a role in the exchange rates of that country's currency. **Countries that are less risky are more attractive to foreign investors. This leads to an appreciation of that currency.** If a country is unstable, it scares investors away and leads to a depreciation of the currency. After all, if a country promises a massive return for an investment, but seems like it will collapse in a day, investors will flee to safer investments in other countries.

Productivity: Lastly, we have a country's productivity. As a country becomes more productive, it becomes a more efficient economy. As a result, that productivity tends to be reflected in the tradable goods sector. As productivity increases, it leads to a lower price for domestic products. As the prices of domestic goods fall, demand for domestic goods increases. Because demand for domestic products is increasing, it leads to an appreciation of the currency in the long run. **So, as a country becomes more productive, its currency**

appreciates. If a country's productivity decreases, the inverse effect will also be observed.

Fixed versus Floating

Throughout the world, there are two general types of currencies. In the foreign exchange market, currencies are classified as fixed currencies and floating rate currencies. Currently, the vast majority of currencies are floating rate currencies. This is what has led to the rise of the forex market and the volatility that can be found within.

Fixed Currency

A fixed currency is a currency that has some form of backing behind it. This gives a form of authority to the currency as it can be tied back to a specific asset. As a result, a fixed currency has very low volatility as each unit of currency is connected to an asset. Domestically, a fixed currency only changes in value when it is manually revalued by the government.

This means that the domestic government has absolute control over the value of a currency in their own markets. This means that the currency's exchange rate with another currency can be determined by what their currency is worth in terms of the value of the asset the fixed currency is tied to. It makes it rather simple to determine the exchange rate, and the exchange rate does not change until the government revalues the currency.

Examples of fixed currencies have been seen throughout history. An extremely popular asset to peg a currency to was precious metals. Most notably, gold and silver were used to back the value of currencies. In the United States, dollars could be exchanged for gold and the government ensured the value of a dollar. In 1973, the gold standard ended in the United States, and the new era of floating currencies began.

I am aware that this is not a history book, but we should at least have a synopsis of how we transitioned into a floating rate currency. During World War II, a bunch of countries got together in 1944 to develop a new method of banking. After all, the massive debts weighing down Germany are what led to the largest war in history. So, a bunch of financial people from different countries got together in a hotel and created the Bretton Woods agreement.

Under the Bretton Woods agreement, it gave the United States the sole right to print dollars. Then all the other countries would peg their currencies to the U.S. dollar. Then they established the World Bank and International Monetary Fund (IMF). All the other countries would then maintain fixed exchange rates between their currency and the dollar. Effectively, all the other countries jumped off the gold standard and tied their currencies to a new asset, the dollar. If a country's currency started to get too low, the IMF would bail them out by acting as a lender. All the countries donated to the IMF, and then they would borrow from it if they had any issues.

So, why did all these countries agree to peg their currencies to the U.S. dollar? Well, because the United States had about three-fourths of the entire world's supply of gold. Basically, all the other countries had hyper inflated their economies so they could fund WW2. The United States was the only stable economy at the time, so they agreed to be the backbone of this experiment. Thus, the entire world shifted from the gold standard to the U.S. dollar standard.

The United States had the dominant currency in the world until 1971. In 1971, the United States was going through a bit of a recession. Naturally, the government decided to inflate the currency a little to combat the recession. Because the currency had inflated, President Nixon decided to devalue the dollar in terms of gold. Now a dollar would be worth 1/38 an ounce of gold instead of 1/35.50 an ounce of gold. Then Nixon devalued it again to 1/42 an ounce of gold per dollar.

So that backfired. People freaked out. They started redeeming their currency for gold and the U.S. started to run out of gold reserves. Additionally, countries started to redeem the dollars they had on hand for gold before the value dropped further. West Germany and Switzerland abandoned the Bretton Woods system in 1971 as well. Finally, Nixon announced that the U.S. would abandon

Bretton Woods and that U.S. dollars could no longer be exchanged for gold.

At this point, the dollar became a fiat currency. A fiat currency is any currency that is given value because of the people that are backing it. In simple terms, fiat is backed by the faith people have in that currency's government. Officially, the gold standard was fully abolished in 1973. Currently, there is no country in the world that is still on the gold standard. Central Banks still keep gold in reserve, however, because it still retains value as a medium of exchange in emergency situations.

Floating Currency

Today, most modern countries in the world have a floating currency. A floating currency is not backed by any asset and fluctuates based on demand and supply. In a floating currency system, the exchange rate goes up or down based on the exchange rate factors. Those factors are not as important for a fixed currency because the government sets the value of the currency in that situation.

In a floating currency, the exchange rate is constantly changing, and the exchange rate is set by the forex market. With a floating currency, the central bank of a country is much less likely to attempt to control its exchange rate. That being said, a central bank may interfere to ensure the stability of the currency and avoid inflation, but it is not a common occurrence. If a country attempts to control their currency too much, it may lead to people not trusting the true exchange rate of the currency.

While an argument can be made that a fixed currency is more stable, it has been disproven by the forex market. In forex, the mark of a truly stable currency is the fact that it maintains its value even while floating. If a currency maintains its value over long periods of time in a floating market, it shows that investors trust that currency to hold value over time. Additionally, fixed currencies are difficult to maintain in the long-term, and they often require the government to revalue the currency regularly to maintain the market rate of the currency. If panic sets in before a country can revalue its currency, the currency can devalue rapidly.

This happened in Thailand in 1997. Up until this point, the Thailand baht had been pegged to the U.S. dollar. Thailand had become over leveraged and had borrowed significantly to maintain their currency value. As a result, Thailand was low on reserves and decided to devalue their currency in relation to the U.S dollar. This stoked fears that the baht had become worth much less than the current pegged rate. People began to convert their bahts into dollars, but Thailand did not have the reserves to meet the demand. The drop in the currency value sent shockwaves throughout other Asian countries. In response to mounting global pressure, Thailand converted into a floating currency. At the time, the baht was pegged to the dollar at 25 baht per U.S. dollar. After becoming a floating currency, the baht fell to 56 baht per U.S. dollar. Thailand received $17 billion in relief from the IMF and started off the Asian financial crisis.

Unfortunately, several countries underwent severe events like this before switching to a floating currency. Mexico was another example that saw its currency drop in value by almost 30% when it was finally forced to switch to a floating currency.

Regardless of the past switches to a floating currency, we now have every major currency listed as a floating currency. This allowed the world to see that it takes the strongest financial systems in order to maintain a floating currency. If a currency fluctuates greatly, then the forex market will be able to show how unstable the currency actually is. If a country is able to maintain their foreign exchange rate over long periods of time, then it shows that their economy is strong and stable.

Who uses the Forex Markets and Why?

In the forex market, there are many different entities that use it to conduct business, control exchange rates, and speculate on future value. These entities are banks, hedge funds, corporations, and individuals. While there may be thousands of entities in the forex market, there are usually only three reasons that someone would want to move in this market. Those are to hedge against a risk, control and manipulate a currency, or speculation.

Central Banks: In the forex market, a central bank represents their country's government. The goal of a central bank is to control and manipulate their home currency. Specifically, the central bank will undergo policies to strengthen, stabilize, or weaken their currency to fit their current needs. When a central bank is manipulating their currency, they are usually trying to make either their imports or exports more competitive in the domestic and global market. Remember, the central bank of a country has complete control over the supply of that currency.

Commercial and Investment Banks: While a central bank represents a country, commercial and investment banks are for-profit entities that use the forex market to hedge their foreign exchange risk. For example, many banks do not operate only in the domestic markets. Many banks make loans to foreign businesses and other countries. When these loans are made, the banks often receive payment in a foreign currency. If the exchange rate suddenly rises or drops, the bank could be exposed to a massive loss or gain. As a result, banks hedge some of their risk by buying or selling the foreign currency to offset a potential loss. Additionally, banks often facilitate transactions for clients. These clients may be conducting speculative trades, and it is the bank's responsibility to mitigate its own risks. Commercial and investment banks use the forex market to hedge against foreign exchange risk and to help other people execute speculative trades.

Corporations: Corporate managers pay a lot of attention to the fluctuations of exchange rates. While the forex market is not relevant for smaller domestic businesses, multinational companies use the forex market to hedge against a sudden downturn in a specific currency. Because the short-term market is almost impossible to predict, companies will often purchase agreements that will hedge their risks in the event that a market change occurs. By operating in the forex market, companies are able to lock in payments for goods and services sold or obtained in other countries. For example, assume that a Japanese car company purchases its materials from China and sells cars in France. The Japanese currency is yen, but China uses the yuan and France uses the euro. The Japanese company would have to purchase Chinese parts by converting their yen into the yuan. Once the materials were imported, the company would assemble the vehicles and ship them over to France. In order to sell the cars to French consumers, the company will have to take payment in euros and convert those euros into yen. You can imagine the difficult task the financial managers of these companies undergo to balance their foreign exchange risk. This type of risk is referred to as translation risk. Assume in the above situation, the Chinese yuan suddenly strengthened against the yen. Suddenly, the Japanese company would realize that the price of the goods they were purchasing were increasing. Initially, they may decide to increase the price of the vehicles that they sell. This can backfire, however, because the price increase may cause consumers in France to not purchase their products. Additionally, the euro may suddenly weaken against the yen. This is problematic if the company is attempting to obtain their hard-earned yen. After all, the French consumer may be paying for a vehicle in euros that are now worth less than they were previously. While the Japanese company loses in both these situations, the reverse may also occur. Regardless of which way that the exchange rate moves, the company wants to secure their future costs and revenues. Using the forex market, they can purchase futures (Chapter 6) that go up in value when a negative exchange rate event occurs. Because so many companies are affected by changing exchange rates, there is a huge market willing to accommodate these risk avoidance strategies. While the Japanese automobile manufacturer was a simple example, the real world gets much more complicated. In the given example, we assumed that all the materials they purchased were from one country and not multiple countries. We even assumed that they were only selling their cars in one country instead of several.

Hopefully, you have a better understanding of the challenges that managers face when running multinational corporations and why the forex market is such an important tool that they use to hedge their exposure to exchange rate risks.

Hedge Funds: In the forex world, the largest players are the banks. The second largest group, however, are the hedge funds. Investment managers at hedge funds often execute speculative forex trades to turn a profit. Many investors turn to hedge funds to make them money. Some of these hedge funds may even only trade in the forex market. They often undergo risky trading strategies to grow their portfolio and make money for the investors. While they often hedge their risk, they can still lose money on individual trades. For example, if a hedge fund makes a bet that a currency will go down in price, they will also make a smaller bet that the currency will increase in price. This way they will not lose as much in the event of their bet being incorrect. They make these bets using futures and options (Chapter 6 and 7). Even though hedge funds may be hedging their investments, it is still extremely speculative. As a result, hedge funds fall into the category of speculative traders, not traders looking to hedge a position.

Individuals: Lastly, who can forget about the individual? Individual investors make up the smallest portion of the forex markets. While individual investors may claim to be using some form of fundamental analysis to place trades, it is more likely that they are day trading and basing their trades on the changing price fluctuations. For the vast majority of individuals, there is no need for them to hedge against any specific currency risk. Therefore, individuals use the forex market for largely speculative trades.

Other Types of Currency Systems

After Bretton Woods ended in 1971, there were still attempts to return to the system that had once dominated the world economy. As a result, several different methods of currency policy began to emerge. Many of these are still used in the modern world and have an impact on the global economy.

Why haven't these alternate forms of economic policy been mentioned before? Because these types of policies are all a form of fixed currency. While none of these currencies are backed by precious metals, they have still fixed themselves to a specific asset. These "other types of currencies" are really just fixed currencies with extra steps.

Each of these fixed currencies can be broken down further into separate categories. To save time, we will only be discussing what these categories are, and avoid listing the various countries that use these systems. Naturally, example countries will be provided, but this is by no means a comprehensive list.

No legal tender: Some countries are too small or don't have a strong enough economy to support their own currency. What do you do when you don't feel like managing your own economic system? Easy, you just use someone else's. That's what countries with no legal tender use. This way they at least get to choose which country's currency they will accept. Some countries have elected to use the U.S. dollar, Euro, or the Australian dollar. Ultimately, the value of these currencies fluctuates with the decisions that other countries make. These countries have decided that operating a currency carries more cons than pros and instead have outsourced that problem to another country.

Currency Board: A currency board is a method that countries use to stabilize their currency. In a country with a currency board, power to control the money supply and exchange rate is taken away from the central bank and given to the currency board. The currency board, however, is still a fixed currency and their currency is still pegged to another country's currency. The currency board will then purchase reserves of the base currency to use as their "gold." Some currency boards have 100% reserve requirements. This means that if the currency board wants to print more money, they have to purchase more of the base currency to maintain their current exchange rate. Additionally, a currency board allows for any exchange between the domestic pegged currency and the foreign base currency. This is very similar to the gold standard, but now the base currency is what the domestic currency can be exchange for instead of gold. Currency boards have to select what they want their base currency to be. In Hong Kong, the currency board uses the U.S. dollar as the base currency, and in Bulgaria, the Euro is used as the exchange rate anchor. While some currency boards are still in use today, past disasters have led to a decline in their popularity throughout the world. One disaster was Argentina's currency board. In April 1st, 1991, Argentina created a currency board that lasted until January 6th, 2002. Argentina's currency board was supposed to be a one for one match to the U.S. dollar. While Argentina had many of the above rules in place, a fixed exchange rate, full convertibility between the other currency, and a fully backed reserve with the foreign currency, they broke all the rules. They violated the rules badly, and it led to a massive financial recession. Regardless of the rule violations, the ultimate cause of the currency board collapse was the appreciation of the U.S. dollar in the late 1990s. As the dollar appreciated, it caused the Argentinian peso to appreciate as well. As a result, the Argentinian currency became overvalued and Argentinian exports became less competitive in the global economy. As exports became less competitive, the economy began to slow down and a recession occurred. Making matters worse, Argentina's government had a large budget deficit for several years. Naturally, they raised taxes to offset the deficit, but it led to an even worse recession. Foreign investors started fleeing the country and moving their money anywhere else. After $20 billion dollars of capital had fled the country, the interest rate for the peso offered by the government was between 50% to 60% to attract foreign investors. The government even went so far as to freeze bank deposits to stop the bleeding. Finally, after an almost four-year recession, the currency board was abolished, and the Argentinian peso switched to a floating currency. Unfortunately, the crisis in Argentina was not an isolated incident. A similar situation occurred in Hong Kong which made the Asian financial crisis even worse. The difference being that Hong Kong's currency board is still in effect today.

Conventional Peg: A conventional peg is very similar to a currency board and the gold standard. The difference being that there is not a currency board and there is no gold. Effectively, the Central Bank takes over the role of the currency board. Just like a currency board, the exchange rate is pegged to a base currency. In the same way, the base currency acts as the "gold" for the country. The domestic currency, however, cannot be exchanged for the base currency at any time. With a strong base currency, an unstable domestic currency can become more stable and start to attract foreign investors. A conventional peg is more popular than a currency board in the global economy. Countries like Aruba, Qatar, and Saudi Arabia use the U.S. dollar as their peg. Similarly, countries like Benin, Chad, and Niger use the Euro as their peg.

Crawling Peg/Pegged Exchange Rate Within Horizontal Bands: In a crawling peg, the country is attempting to develop a stable currency, but also allow the currency to fluctuate. Similar to all other fixed currencies, the crawling peg has a domestic pegged currency and a foreign base currency. The crawling peg was developed to solve the rigidity that the conventional peg had. In a conventional peg, the base currency can appreciate or depreciate. When that occurs, it can have disastrous consequences for the domestic economy of the pegged currency. The crawling peg attempts to solve this problem by having a band of exchange rates. In effect, the exchange rate is allowed to fluctuate within a range of rates. Some crawling pegs are set to adjust at a fixed rate and time, and others are simply adjusted whenever it is needed. Of course, the government can adjust these bands to fit the current state of affairs. In order to ensure that its currency remains within the bands, the country may buy or sell its own currency to keep the exchange rate where they want it. The crawling peg has become unpopular in recent years due to the difficulty associated with maintaining a stable currency when outside forces try to manipulate the currency. As a result, there are very few examples of countries that use a crawling peg. Currently, Nicaragua and Botswana both use crawling pegs.

Crawl-Like Peg: Much more popular than the crawling peg, many countries have adopted a "crawl-like peg." These are honestly extremely similar to the crawling peg with one key difference. That difference is what the IMF classifies a country to be. Specifically, a craw-like arrangement is not explicitly stated, but the currency acts in a way that the IMF believes it to be crawl-like. To be classified as crawl-like, a currency must remain in a stable pattern within a 2% change for six months or more. Additionally, the currency must appreciate or depreciate in a "monotonic and continuous manner." Basically, these currencies don't fit the category of a crawling peg, but the currency appears to be stable during longer periods of time. Often times, these arrangements are still pegged to another currency, but it is a looser peg.

Forex Throughout the Years

Assuming that you haven't stopped reading out of boredom, we should talk about some of the crazy events that have been caused by the forex market. While the forex market is relatively stable in the long run, the periods of instability make the best stories. Here are a few of the events that have been brought about by the forex market.

To start, we would be remiss if we didn't mention Black Wednesday. September 16th, 1992 is the day that the UK refers to as Black Wednesday. For many forex traders, however, it is known as the day that George Soros "broke" the Bank of England. After the dust settled, Soros had made over $1 billion and cemented himself as one of the most incredible forex traders in history.

We need to understand what happened before 1992 to lead up to this legendary event. In 1976, European countries that had united underneath the European union were attempting to reconcile the fact that every single country had their own currency. They had not yet created the euro, and they were attempting to keep all of their currencies tied to each other. So, they all got together and tied exchange rates to each other's currencies. Then they had the central banks of each country artificially maintain the value of these currencies to avoid fluctuations between the various European countries.

They called their plan the European Rate Mechanism (ERM). Interestingly, the UK wasn't fond of the ERM and didn't want to join in the beginning. Eventually, the UK saw how other currencies were performing extremely well and decided to join. After being in the ERM for two years, the British pound started to depreciate in value. If the pound depreciated too quickly, then Britain would be forced to leave the ERM because they would fall below the requirement to be in the ERM.

As the pound was depreciating, the Bank of England (BoE) became defensive. They raised interest rates to bring in investors, and they started buying back pounds using foreign reserves to raise the exchange rate. On the other side, George Soros became offensive. Soros took out a large short position against the pound. Specifically, Soros felt that the pound was overvalued against the German Mark. In his short position, he exchanged the pound for the deutsche mark. He also believed the Bank of England did not have enough foreign currency reserves to buy back the pound if it were to go down in value.

Then, George Soros began to publicly give his sentiment about how he felt about the overvalued pound. Other financial managers took notice and also placed bets against the pound. Naturally, this pressure had to be met by the Bank of England. As more and more investors started to fear the collapse of the pound, it led to panic. Businesses and speculators started betting against the pound to both hedge their risk and make money.

A day before Black Wednesday, the war began. At 8:30 A.M. the BoE executed two 300 million-pound orders to buy back the pound. Soros also started to sell large amounts of the pound on the forex market. In the same day, the UK announced two interest rate increases. One to 12% from 10% and another to 15% in the afternoon. Naturally, a 50% increase in the interest rate did not go over well with society. Speculators began pushing back and continued to bet against the pound. At 7:00 P.M. the UK officially announced that they would leave the ERM because they were unable to maintain the value of their currency.

Then, September 16th came. The Bank of England had been broken and the pound started a free fall. In one day, the pound fell 15% against the deutsche mark and 25% against the U.S. dollar. Soros' hedge fund gained over $1 billion in one day. While the general public did not benefit in any way from this event, a bunch of financial managers became extremely wealthy. Ultimately, the ERM became known as a failed policy that severely damaged the UK's reputation. The BoE officially lost $3.3 billion trying to stabilize their currency.

This event became the example for how unwise and futile it is to interfere with the market. If the market has a negative sentiment for your currency, it does not matter how many billions of dollars you use to stabilize your currency. Your currency will move along with what the market determines. In the case of the United Kingdom, a distrust of the UK government combined with a lack of faith in the Bank of England and an overvalued currency led to Black Wednesday. A day that lives in infamy in the UK.

Another story is that of Stanley Druckenmiller. Stanley actually worked for George Soros while the bank was being broken.

Specifically, Druckenmiller followed Soros' bet by buying British stocks and buying German bonds. Stanley felt that the British government would eventually have to cut back on their interest rates which would devalue the pound. If the pound fell in value, then it would help British businesses that were exporting to other countries because those companies could become more competitive in price with a cheaper pound. In simple terms, a weaker pound would help British exports and the companies that were exporting.

The other side of the trade were the German bonds that he purchased. If the deutsche mark became stronger in comparison to the pound, then German stocks would slow in growth. If stock growth slowed down, then investors would turn to bonds to receive similar rates of return. While these were side bets against the pound, they considerably helped add to the profits made on the pound short.

Previously to the breaking of the Bank of England, Druckenmiller had made another bet that the deutsche mark would appreciate in value. When the Berlin Wall was falling, the deutsche mark had fallen in value significantly because of the difficulties associated with reuniting West and East Germany. Stanley felt that the depreciated mark was too extreme. As a result, he placed a bet that the currency would rise in value in the future. Initially, he put in a few million that the mark would rally. George Soros saw the trade and told Druckenmiller to increase the trade to $2 billion. He did, and the trade helped the fund make a 60% return for the year. Stanley Druckenmiller is a legend that is known for betting on the deutsche mark twice and winning both times.

The last story in this section covers Andrew Krieger. Krieger was an aggressive trader that repeatedly impressed the management at his firm. He impressed them so much that they gave him a $700 million trading limit. For reference, others in the firm only had a $50 million trading limit. While most institutional investors at this time made investments in the $20 million to $25 million range, Krieger was known for making $250 million trades regularly.

During the time that Krieger was working with this large amount of capital, the stock market experienced an event that went down in history as Black Monday. On October 19, 1987, the stock market fall in value by more than 20% in a single day. While the cause of the crash has never been made clear, many people believe that it had to do with new computer programs that overwhelmed the NYSE with sell orders. This caused investors to panic and led to one of the worst crashes the stock market had ever seen.

While the world was recoiling from the sudden drop, investors started to look for "safe" currencies. In effect, many investors were fearful of the U.S. dollar and were fleeing to other currencies. As a result, demand for foreign currencies is increasing. As the demand for a currency goes up, the value of the currency increases, and the exchange rate goes up in comparison to other currencies. Remember that these changes are usually short-term and not long-term effects.

This sudden increase in the value of foreign currencies caught Krieger's attention. Specifically, Krieger focused on the kiwi. No, I am not talking about the fruit. The kiwi is the official currency of New Zealand. Because the value of the kiwi had suddenly increased in a day, Krieger viewed the currency as being overvalued. Armed with this belief and a $700 million trading limit, Krieger chose to short the kiwi.

Using options (Chapter 7) Krieger was able to heavily leverage himself to execute a massive trade. It is believed that Krieger's leverage was at 400 to 1. Because he had such a massive leverage, it is believed that Krieger was shorting more than the entire money supply of New Zealand. Yes, Krieger was likely shorting more kiwis than the combined total of all kiwis on the market.

Because the kiwi had risen so quickly, the market had to correct itself to return to normal. Shortly after, the kiwi dropped in value by 5%. Krieger exited the trade and made a $300 million profit. Krieger eventually left the company he was working for because he felt his bonus was not large enough and went on to work with George Soros.

These are some fun stories that people like to read because of the incredible nature and power that the forex seems to hold over a currency. These stories are certainly exceptional and are not the norm in the industry, but they are fun to learn about and appreciate the risks these people were willing to take to turn a profit.

How Traders Buy and Sell Foreign Currencies

So now that we understand the basic fundamentals and history of the foreign exchange market, we can start looking at how traders actually buy and sell these currencies. When referring to the foreign exchange market, traders often refer to the spot market or the forward/futures/option market. While we will cover what the second market is in later chapters, we should understand what traders are referring to when they discuss these topics.

In the spot market, investors physically purchase and sell various currencies. The price is determined by the exchange rate at the time. In a typical spot market transaction, one party exchanges currency to another party for the other party's currency at a set rate. So, if I need to exchange my U.S. dollars for Japanese yen, I would perform a spot transaction and exchange my dollars for someone else's yen. The rate would be set as we enter into the transaction, and then we would exchange currencies. Both parties receive the currency of their choice and the position closes.

Typically, a spot trade can take about two days before it officially settles. This market has become very popular for individuals and speculators.

In the futures market, however, the actual currency is not traded. Instead, a derivative is traded that represents a future claim to a currency. These derivatives are based on the spot market, and they go up and down in value depending on the exchange rates of each respective currency. We will go into more detail on these derivatives later and the differences between each of them. Companies are more attracted to the futures market because it allows them to hedge their currency exchange risk. Unless you are a hedge fund, the futures market is primarily used to hedge against risks rather than turn a profit.

Interestingly enough, traders will almost never actually take physical control of the currency. In the case of the spot market, currencies will never leave their bank accounts until they are exchanged for something else. In the futures market, traders will usually sell the future to another investor before its term expires. As a result, traders may never actually see the asset they are trading.

When traders are discussing what they are trading, they often refer to forex pairs. A forex pair is a pair of two currencies that is quoted at an exchange rate. In a forex pair, there is a base currency and a quote currency. Here is an example of a forex pair.

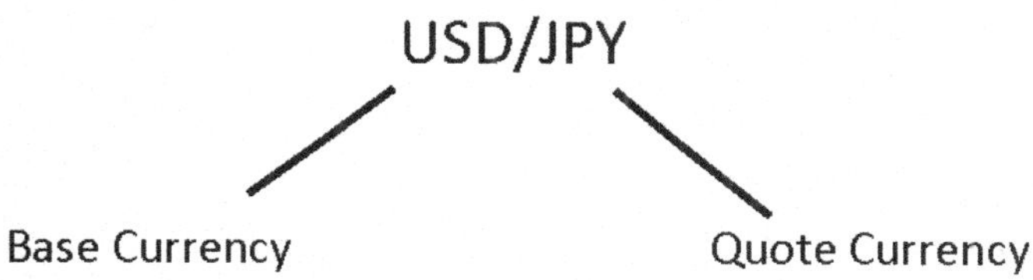

Here, our base currency is USD, and our quote currency is JPY. In a forex pair, the base currency always comes first, and the quote currency always comes last. Once you view a forex pair, there is a bid/ask price that is associated with the currency. A bid price is the price that traders sell at and the ask price is the price that traders buy at. Wait a minute, why is there a difference between what investors can buy and sell the currency at? Well, banks have to make money on facilitating transactions somehow. This is how they do it. Typically, a forex pair will have a lower bid price than ask price. Meaning that if you buy a currency, you cannot immediately sell it to make your money back. You would actually receive less than your originally exchanged amount. As a result, when trading forex there are two prices that traders are given and knowing the difference between them is key.

To continue our example, say that the forex pair we are looking at is the U.S. dollar and the Japanese yen. So, we would want to see the bid and ask prices between the two currencies.

USD/JPY

Bid: 108.77

Ask: 108.8

Again, traders can ask to exchange USD at a rate of 108.8, and they can sell their JPY at 108.77. Traders will often refer to the spread in a forex pair. The spread is the difference between the bid and ask price on any currency pair. Sometimes the spread on a currency transaction can be so small that traders use pips to measure the movements between currencies.

A pip is measured by each movement in the fourth decimal point. So, one pip would be equal to 0.0001. In the Japanese currency, pips are actually the second decimal point which would be 0.01. This is only for JPY transactions. Every other major currency uses pips in 0.0001. In the above example, if the exchange rate changed from 108.77 to 108.76, then the exchange rate has moved one pip.

For every other forex pair that does not include JPY, the pip is measured in 0.0001. In these cases, a movement from 25 to 25.0001 would be one pip. Forex investors watch these price changes with great interest as it can make or break their investments.

One technique in forex that takes advantage of these seemingly miniscule price changes is arbitrage. In the financial world, arbitrage is any trade that would be risk-free and guarantee a profit. In currency arbitrage, traders take advantage of pricing inefficiencies between forex pairs. By taking advantage of these inefficiencies, traders can make a guaranteed profit. In order to take advantage of an arbitrage opportunity, real time pricing must be available to the trader and the trader must act extremely quickly before the market corrects itself.

Here is an example of an arbitrage trade. In order to execute one of these trades, the trader is usually looking at three forex pairs to complete this transaction. For our example, we will be using EUR/USD, EUR/JPY, and JPY/USD. The exchange rates will be 1.1942, 130.18, and 0.0092 respectively.

EUR/USD: 1.1942

EUR/JPY: 130.18

JPY/USD: 0.0092

To start, we will spend $23,884 to obtain 20,000 euros. With those 20,000 euros, we will exchange them for 2,603,600 yen. With the 2,603,600 yen, we will exchange them for $23,953.12. This yields a profit of $69.12.

Naturally, a professional trader could do this with a much larger amount. Once the trader has exploited the pricing inefficiency, the market will often correct itself. Often times, computers automatically execute these transactions at speeds faster than any trader could even locate and exploit them. While the profit experienced on this trade might seem insignificant, keep in mind that this profit occurred in a matter of seconds and was likely executed by a computer before the market could even hope to correct itself. With enough of these opportunities and a large amount of capital, large amounts of money stand to be made.

Hopefully, you have gained an understanding of the forex market and can identify the various factors and aspects of the forex market that investors look at. The forex market is a fast-paced market that never stops. It is intriguing in its complexity and our lack of general understanding towards short-term price changes. Its unpredictability is the focus of study for professional researchers, large corporations, and speculators alike.

6.

Forwards/Futures

Now that we have walked through the world of stocks, bonds and currencies, we can focus on the wonderful futures market. Futures can be difficult for people to understand. The best way to explain what a future does is to describe it alongside other market instruments that we have already discussed. If a stock represents partial ownership in a company and a bond represents a debt that a company owes to an investor, **then a future is a contract**. In effect, all futures are contracts that have been set between various parties to control and predict the price of a good listed on the future.

Someone who owns a future contract does not actually yet own the underlying asset that is written on the contract. Instead, they own a contract that **requires them** to buy or sell that asset at a set future date and at a set future price. It should be noted, that a futures contract **requires** the parties to buy or sell the asset at the set price. If you are still confused, its fine. We are going to walk you through exactly how a future works and why they are so widely used. Remember that a future is a contract between two parties. Nothing more and nothing less.

Before we jump into a discussion about futures contracts and the various differences between them, we should first discuss how futures even came about in the first place. The futures market can actually be traced back to the middle ages. Keep in mind that some of these markets were active in some way back in the 1500s. Eventually, a modern exchange was established in 1710 in Japan. Later, in 1877 another modern exchange was established in London. So, these markets have existed for hundreds of years, but why would people need futures contracts in the 1500s?

Pretend that you are a poor wheat farmer living in the 1500s. You work hard all year just so that you can sell your wheat at the market after your harvest. Unfortunately, you have absolutely no control over what the price of wheat will be when you go to sell it. If you are lucky, wheat will be in high demand and you will be able to make more money than normal. If you are unlucky, however, there will be an oversupply of wheat which requires you to sell your wheat at the cheapest possible price just to get rid of it.

Clearly, there is a dilemma. As a farmer, you cannot predict what the price of wheat will be. What if there was a way that you could know for certain what the price of wheat would be? Enter in, a future contract. In this case, the contract would require you to sell your wheat at a set price in the future. The price is set once you enter into the contract. If the market price of wheat is higher than your contracted amount when you go to sell, then you will lose out on some of the money you could have made selling your wheat at market prices. If the market price of wheat is lower, however, the future contract may allow you to be more profitable than you would have been otherwise.

Well, that applies to the broke farmer back in the day, but what about today? Today, futures contracts are more important than ever before. In the past, futures were limited to farm products. Now, futures include commodities, currencies, stock prices, and bond prices. Additionally, futures are now traded on exchanges that have standardized the process of exchanging goods. The exchanges have set the rules and govern the way that futures transactions are carried out. In order to buy a future, you must go through an organized exchange. Typically, futures are most popular for produced commodities that have fluctuating prices from month to month.

What exactly is a commodity? A commodity is considered to be a basic good. Typically, commodities are raw materials that are used to produce something else. For example, the coffee that you buy at a coffee shop is not a commodity. The coffee beans that were used to make the coffee, however, is an actively traded future and a commodity. A car is not a commodity. Instead, the oil which allows the car to run smoothly is a commodity.

Especially important in the futures markets are now companies. It is no longer focused on the poor farmer that needs to secure their earnings for the coming year. Now, companies use the futures markets to hedge the risks that they are exposed to when purchasing raw materials to produce products.

Pretend for a moment that you are a large construction company that is reliant on lumber to build houses. If you enter into a contract to build a house and the price of lumber suddenly rises, you may go out of business or lose an immense amount of money building the house. As a result, you may decide to enter into a future contract to buy lumber at a set price in the future. As you can see, the futures market plays an important role in the business operations of many companies.

Categories of Commodities

Before we jump into the various types of futures and the differences between them, we should understand the various types of commodities that are exchanged in futures contracts. Keep in mind that there are a lot of futures that do not trade any type of commodity. Instead, they may have another underlying asset that gives them value. To keep things simple for now, we are focusing on futures that deal with commodities. Below, there is a chart with the various categories of commodities that are traded in commodity futures and some examples to go along with them.

Hard Commodities Natural resources that must be obtained by mining or extracting.		**Soft Commodities** Agricultural products like livestock or plants.	
Metal	Energy	Livestock	Agriculture
-gold	-oil	-pork	-corn
-silver	-water	-beef	-wheat
-copper	-coal	-eggs	-soybeans
-platinum	-electricity		-coffee

Aspects of a Future Contract

While there are many different types of futures contracts, there are several unifying aspects that investors look at when evaluating whether to buy or sell a future. In a contract, the buyer and seller agree on a specified price, quantity, and date when that product will be delivered. When the contracted date arrives, the product is delivered, and the set price is paid for the commodity.

As a general rule, the party that is delivering the asset will file a “notice of intention to deliver” with the exchange. This notice will specify the grade of the asset being brought and the delivery location.

It should be noted that most futures contracts are sold to larger buyers, and futures positions are typically closed out before taking physical delivery of the commodity. As a result, the vast majority of futures contracts that are initiated do not resolve in a delivery to the person who initially opened the position. Someone does buy them, but many people close out of their positions before taking delivery. Below are the various aspects of a standard future.

The Asset: In every single futures contract, there is an underlying asset that the contract is based on. In the above text, we spoke about commodities as a common underlying asset. So, an oil future will have an underlying asset of oil. As the value of oil rises or falls, then the value of the future also rises and falls. Other underlying assets are stocks, currencies, indexes, and even interest rates. We will explore these types of futures later, but for now let's focus on commodities. Often times, commodity futures will specify the exact grade or quality that the underlying asset must be when it is delivered. If the quality of the asset is not up to the specified standard when it is delivered, it can affect the price that is paid upon delivery. In extreme cases, the entire order may be cancelled, and the money invested into the future refunded. Usually, in non-commodity futures a grade is typically not specified.

Contract Size: In a futures contract, the size of the delivered asset is extremely important. There is a big difference between 1 pound and 20 metric tons. A contract size that specifies a few metric tons is not uncommon in a futures contract. The size of the contract specifies the amount on an asset that is to be delivered in one contract. A standardized exchange has an important decision to make when deciding how large to make the contracted size. If the contracted size is too large, then it may be difficult for companies to properly hedge their risk using futures. If the amount of product a company needs to hedge is too small, it may not make sense for a company to even use a futures contract. If a contract is too small, however, suppliers may not want to use them either because they would have to transport small amounts of product for each contract. Exchanges are constantly looking to hit that perfect sweet spot for each contract when they are drafting it and presenting it to investors.

Contract length: The length of a contract is important for investors looking to buy a future. The length of the contract specifies on which month the contract will expire. Similar to contract size, the length of a contract is set by an exchange. Also, the exchange has to take into consideration the potential needs of its investors. If a contract length is too long or short, it can lead to a lack of desire to use futures as a hedge to risk.

Delivery Location: Because futures are traded on a standardized exchange, the exchange will have locations set up where physical delivery of the asset can occur. Even though most traders close out of their positions and never take delivery of the asset, these locations are provided for the times when physical delivery does occur. The exchange will even require that certain commodities be delivered to specific locations. For example, did you know that you can buy an orange juice future? Specifically, the Intercontinental Exchange (ICE) has an orange juice future contract that is active today. If you are looking for 15,000 pounds of orange juice to be delivered to you, you can buy one of these futures. The delivery location for this commodity, however, is to licensed warehouses in Florida, New Jersey, and Delaware. As a result, the contract clearly states that the orange juice must be delivered to and picked up from this location. Nobody is going to deliver this to a front door. Investors need to go and pick this up themselves.

Delivery Date: Futures contracts are referred to by their respective delivery month. So, when a company wants to purchase a corn future for December, they would purchase a December corn future. For many futures, the delivery date of the asset is the whole month. If you own a future contract, you will want to pay attention to the last day that a contract can be traded. Exchanges will specify the first day when a contract can start trading as well as the last day that the contract can be traded. A contract will stop being traded a few days before the last day that a delivery can be made.

Margin

Now that we know what the different aspects of a futures contract look like, we can learn about what investors go through when buying a contract. Specifically, we can focus on the concept of margin. Margin was previously discussed in Chapter 2. There, we learned that investors have the option to purchase shares of a company on margin. Margin is like borrowing money to make your investments. It can allow investors to make higher than normal returns by using other people's money, but it exposes them to a higher risk factor.

While margin was an important concept to understand when discussing the risks associated with investing with borrowed money, it was not a requirement to understand the various concepts in the stock market. After all, it is the investor's decision whether to invest using margin. In the futures market, however, **margin is a requirement**. In fact, not only is margin a requirement, but the requirements to use margin are much **less** restrictive than the stock market.

As you may recall, when purchasing a company's stock on margin it is required that the investor put up at least 50% of the capital that is used in the purchase. Some brokers may have higher requirements, but the lowest any broker is legally allowed to go is 50%. In the futures market, the exchanges are allowed to set their own margin requirements. The exchanges can and often do set their margin requirements at 5% or 10% of the tradable contract. This means that an investor can leverage their position at a ratio of 10:1 or 20:1. So, if you have $10,000 and the margin requirement is 5%, you could enter into a $200,000 futures contract. While this is how the exchanges typically operate, they can change the margin requirements at any time. So, if the market is volatile, they may raise the margin requirement to hedge their own risk.

Similar to margin in the stock market, organized exchanges also use a maintenance margin for their accounts. The maintenance margin is a set dollar amount that the exchange sets for the account. At the end of each trading day, the margin account is adjusted for any gain or loss during the day. This is referred to as "daily settlement" and is standard across many exchanges. If the value of the account falls below the maintenance margin, then the investor will receive a margin call. During a margin call, the investor has the option to post the additional margin or close out of the position.

As an illustration, say that Chad Thompson decides to enter into 10 futures contracts that has a total initial margin of $5,000 and a maintenance margin of $3,500. Each contract is worth $3,000. So, the total value of the account is $30,000. So, Chad enters into the contracts and posts his initial margin. One month later, Chad receives a phone call. Ring ring, the exchange is calling, and the value in his account dropped to $2,100. Chad is now faced with the decision of keeping his account open or putting more money in his account. So, Mr. Thompson doubles down and gets his account back to $5,000 with an additional $2,900. With additional funds, the exchange keeps his account open and the trade active.

How did Chad get to this point? Well, in order to get to $2,100, he had to witness a drop in the value of his investment. The drop, however, is much smaller than you would initially think. In a normal investment, we would say that the value dropped by 58%. (2,100 – 5,000)/5,000

In this example, however, Chad was levered on a scale of 6:1. So in reality, the value of the future contract only dropped by 9.6667%. While this is still a significant drop, it is nowhere near as significant as the 58% that we saw earlier. Instead of his account dropping to $2,100, what if his account had fallen to $3,400, right below the maintenance margin? He would still receive a margin call, and all it would take would be a 5.333% drop in the underlying asset. If Chad decided not to provide the additional funds, the exchange would liquidate his account and close out the position. Hopefully this serves as an example that margin is a useful tool with potentially disastrous consequences.

Exiting a Position

Now that we have covered buying a future, we can look at the options investors have when selling their positions. In a contract, there is a specified expiration date. This is the last date that the contract can be traded. Each exchange will decide what that date is, but it is often times the third Friday of the expiration month. Specific contracts may differ, and investors should always check before entering into a contract. Regardless, investors have three options when choosing to exit out of a futures contract.

Offsetting the Position: This is the most common method of exiting a contract and it is the easiest to understand. Using this method, a trader does not have to take physical delivery of the asset. Here, the trader takes out an opposite and equal transaction in order to neutralize the trade. Because this is all occurring on a centralized exchange, the exchange recognizes the neutralizing contracts and does not require the investor to physically obtain the asset. For example, Jackeline Figueredo decides to go long on 5 steel futures. Later, she decides that it's time to exit her position. At that point, she will short 5 of the exact same contracts that expire on the same date. The difference between the initial position and the offset position are the profit or loss on the trade.

Rollover: A rollover is less of an exit strategy and more of a continuation of what was already occurring. In a rollover, the trader will move their position to expire on another contract in the future. It's almost like the trader is pushing back the expiration date of the contract. In a rollover, the trader will offset their current position and then purchase new contracts that expire in a different month. So, if Jackeline decides that she is doing great and thinks that she can continue to make money on the same trade, she may consider a rollover. To keep things simple, let's pretend that she has been long on her 5 steel futures. To perform the rollover, Jackeline will offset her position by shorting her five steel futures. Then, she simultaneously purchases 5 more long steel futures that expire on a further away date.

Settlement: This is the final form of exiting a futures contract, and it is less of an exit strategy and more like simply taking physical delivery of the asset. If a trader never offset their position or rolled it over before the expiration date, then the trade will go into settlement. At this point, the asset will be prepared to be delivered and the buyer of the contract needs to go pick it up.

Measuring the Value of a Contract

Investors need to understand how the value of their contracts are determined and what measurements are used when the price changes. For this, investors need to use the contract size, tick size, current price, and purchase price.

The first thing that investors need to look at is the current value of the contract. This can actually be confusing because of the way that prices are quoted on exchanges. For example, coffee futures may be quoted at 155.35. **This quote is not in dollars.** That is simply the number of points that the contract is worth. In futures, quotes are measured in points and ticks. If you remember, the foreign exchange market uses pips as the smallest unit of measurement. In futures, the smallest unit of measurement is the tick.

A tick is considered to be the smallest price movement that the market will record. Here's the thing, every single market uses their own measurement for a tick. In gold futures, the tick is 0.1. Coffee futures use a tick size of 0.05 and crude oil has a tick size of 0.01. It is important to carefully watch each market for their designated tick size.

Next up, we have points. A point is actually quoted in dollars. Using the set value of one point, we can multiply the number of points in the quote by the value of one point. With that, we are able to determine what the price of one futures contract will be. Here is an example of a coffee future along with the tick size, tick value, and point value so that what you just read will actually make sense.

Coffee Futures

Quote: 156.30

Tick Size: 0.05

Tick Value: 18.75

Point Value: 1 = $375

Contract Size: 37,500 pounds

Given the above information, we are able to determine the price of the future. For the tick value, it is just the point value divided by the number of ticks it would take to make up one po nt. For this contract, one point would have 20 ticks inside it. Which means that 375 divided by 20 will equal $18.75. Now that we know what each point is worth, we can multiply the value of one point times the quote. We then multiply $375 and 156.30 to obtain $58,612.50. We are now able to understand what the current price of one futures contract is.

On a side note, we can also calculate how much the person buying this contract is paying per pound of coffee. To get this, simply divide the price of the contract by the contract size. Here, we get $58,612.50 divided by 37,500 pounds. This gives us a final price of $1.563 per pound of coffee.

We should now understand how to price futures. You can even look at other futures that you are interested in and apply this information to a contract quote. Now, let's look at how traders calculate their profit and loss on a trade. We will use the same coffee future example in order to keep things simple.

The profit or loss on a future can be easily calculated using the quote at which you purchased a future, subtracted from the quote at which you exited the position, multiplied by the number of futures contracts. For example, an investor purchases 5 coffee futures at 145.6 and decides to sell them at 156.3. To calculate the profit on this trade, subtract 145.6 from 156.3 for a total of 10.7. We can then multiply that 10.7 by $375 to get $4,012.50. This is the increase in value for one contract. We can then multiply this by 5 to get $20,062.50. This would represent the total profit for the transaction. Keep in mind that this does not take into account the initial cost of the investment. Also, futures have bid and ask prices associated with them. This is very similar to the foreign exchange market and the bid and ask prices that they have. Every future contract will also have a cost associated with creating the contract, but we are not looking at that in this example.

Price Limits and Position Limits

For most futures, there are restrictions on how much a future's price can increase or decrease in a day. These restrictions are referred to as price limits. There are both upper and lower price limits that the exchange sets. If the price of a future increases to the upper price limit, the future is said to be limit up. If the price of the future drops to the lower price limit, the future is said to be limit down.

In most cases, when a contract hits a price limit, the trading for the day stops. In special cases, however, the exchange can step in and change the price limits manually. The reason for price limits is to avoid large price swings due to excessive speculative trading. Unfortunately, the limits can also act as a barrier to the true value of the contract when the value of the underlying asset is rising or falling quickly. Whether or not price limits are beneficial to the futures market is debatable and is still controversial to this day.

The other limit that the exchanges will set is a position limit. A position limit is the maximum number of contracts that one investor can hold on a specific future. Position limits are used to prevent any one person from heavily influencing the market. Without position limits, one investor with a few billion dollars could come in and drive the price of a specific future up. That would greatly damage investors on the opposite side of that transaction without the funds to compete. With position limits they are unable to manipulate the market with this tactic.

Before investing in a future, you should be aware of the limits that are set on daily price swings and the limits set on individual positions. These limits are made with the intent of avoiding market manipulation by any one individual and ensuring that the contracts remain stable until expiration.

The Exchanges

It might seem strange that we have not yet covered the exchanges in which these contracts are initiated, traded, and settled. In reality, it is not necessary to understand the various exchanges to understand how a future works. We will cover the role of exchanges in the futures market here. This is fairly straightforward, so this section will be brief.

Unlike the stock market which has only two major exchanges in the United States, there are several exchanges that manage futures in the U.S. The largest being the Chicago Mercantile Exchange (CME), Intercontinental Exchange (ICE), and CBOE Holdings. Keep in mind that these are the largest in the United States. Other large exchanges throughout the world include the National Stock Exchange of India, Eurex, and the Moscow Exchange. Focusing on the United States, however, the exchanges will register with the Commodity Futures Trading Commission (CFTC). This is the regulatory body of the United States that is in charge of monitoring the exchanges based in the United States.

The exchanges facilitate the transactions that occur in this market. They do more, however, than just act as an intermediary. In fact, many of the large exchanges operate their own clearinghouses. Because the exchange sets the rules for the contract, they can require that the sellers deliver to their clearinghouses. Once the delivery is made to the clearinghouse, the buyers have to pick up the assets from the clearinghouse.

The exchanges make money from creating the contracts, but they also generate a significant part of their revenue from their clearinghouses. As a result, clearinghouses make money from both the creation of the contracts and managing the assets for the investors when they arrive.

Speculation vs. Hedging

In this market, there are two main reasons that people enter. The first is to speculate on future price movements in order to turn a profit, and the second is to hedge against some type of risk. While we have briefly mentioned the roles of these two types of investors, a deeper analysis is in order.

To start, let's look at the role of speculators in the futures market. In order to make money in a future's position, speculators can buy low and sell high or even sell high and buy low. Ultimately, a speculator's primary goal is to generate a profit. Speculators come in a variety of forms. A "speculator" can be an individual, a trading firm, portfolio managers, hedge funds, or market makers. All of these speculators should sound familiar to you except for market makers.

Market makers are firms that have contracted with the exchanges to provide liquidity to the markets when they need it.

These firms provide bids and offers continuously in exchange for a reduction of trading fees. These firms are especially important to the futures market because they help facilitate large transactions without changing the price.

Even though a market maker's primary goal is providing liquidity, all speculators provide liquidity to the futures market. Even if unintentional, speculators play a key role in ensuring that futures will have buyers and sellers when the time arises and in keeping the markets as liquid as possible. This benefits all of the players in the market.

Other investors, however, have a serious vested interest in the underlying asset of these contracts. Those investors are the hedgers. A hedger is an individual or firm that actually buys or sells the physical commodity in the future. Hedgers include producers, retailers, wholesalers, or manufacturers. A hedger is constantly affected by the changes in prices. This presents a risk as the landscape of future costs and revenues are unknown. To minimize these risks, hedgers use futures.

There are several types of hedgers in the markets. They often tend to fall on both sides of a contract. There are "buy-side" hedgers and "sell-side" hedgers. On the buy side, there are concerns about rising commodity prices. If prices continue to rise, then they may be forced to raise prices or go out of business. A future can help them mitigate their risk as commodity prices rise.

On the sell side, there are concerns about falling commodity prices. If prices suddenly fall, anybody selling the commodity will experience a loss in revenue. These hedgers have to ensure that the prices of commodities remain stable for the future.

While there is a significant difference between speculators and hedgers, they are both primary participants in the markets. They both play a major role in ensuring the markets function properly and they keep the markets moving at all times.

Futures Trading Terminology

Before we start discussing the various terms that investors use when describing their positions in a future, an important distinction should be made between terms used by individual exchanges and general investment statements. Each and every exchange actually has their own codes that they use to distinguish between various contracts. This book will not cover those codes because they are specific to each exchange and spending time learning about each exchange's codes is time consuming and unnecessary for an understanding of this market. If you would like to learn about a specific exchange's codes, they are publicly disclosed, and you can typically obtain them from their websites.

We will instead be focusing on the ways that a position in a future contract is described. In the futures market, there are only two positions that an investor can take. An investor is only allowed to buy or sell a contract. To keep things simple, an investor buys a contract if they feel that the price of the underlying asset will increase in the future. An investor will sell a contract if they believe that the underlying asset will instead go down in value. So, let's walk through why that is the case.

To start, let's look at buying a contract. As an investor, you believe the price of a specific asset will increase in the future. By purchasing a contract, it requires the investor to purchase an asset at a set price. If the market price of the asset goes higher than the set price in the contract, then the contract increases in value. The reason for this is that the investor is now allowed to purchase the asset at a lower price than the current market rate. The opposite affect can also occur, and the future will instead lose value.

On the other side of the transaction, is the investor selling the asset. In this situation, the investor believes that the price of the asset will decrease in value. By choosing to sell the contract, it requires the investor to sell the asset at a set price. If the market price of the asset falls, then the contract increases in value. The reason for this is that the investor is now allowed to sell the asset at a higher price than the current market price. Naturally, if the market price increases then the value of the contract will fall.

As you can see, contracts are assets that rise and fall in value as the market price of the underlying asset rises and falls. There is a great benefit or liability depending on whether or not the contract requires the investor to buy or sell the underlying asset. You can see how a contract that requires someone to buy an asset at lower than market price would appeal to investors. Below is an example to better understand the effects of buying and selling a future. As you will see, one side tends to "win" and the other will "lose."

Corn Futures

Buying a contract	**Selling a contract**
Contract set price: $0.35/bushel	Contract set price: $0.35/bushel
Future scenarios	**Future scenarios**
Scenario #1	Scenario #1
Market price at contract expiration: $0.40/bushel	Market price at contract expiration: $0.40/bushel
Scenario #2	Scenario #2
Market price at contract expiration: $0.30/bushel	Market Price at contract expiration: $0.30/bushel
Profit or Loss in each scenario	**Profit or Loss in each scenario**
Scenario #1: profit	Scenario #1: loss
Scenario #2: loss	Scenario#2: profit

What affects a Future's Price?

There are several factors that affect a future's price. The most obvious being the demand for the underlying asset that moves the price around. As the price of the underlying asset changes, so does the value of the contract. There are other factors, however, that can impact the price of a contract.

One factor that has historically been observed is the way that the future's price and the spot (market) price change as the expiration date comes closer. It is often observed that on the day of the delivery of the underlying asset, the price of the contract and the price that is being paid in the market are equal to or very close together. So, the farther out that a contract is from expiration, the farther apart the prices tend to be. As the delivery date comes closer, the future's price and the market price also come closer together. Therefore, one can surmise that the greatest profit can be made on a contract the farther out the delivery date is, but the risk of loss is also higher.

Lastly, there is another potential factor that affects the price of a contract. Two famous economists, John Hicks and John Maynard Keynes, once argued that the differences between hedgers and speculators could lead to a lower or higher than expected price for a contract. For example, if hedgers were concerned about a sudden drop in the price of a commodity, they may take out several short positions. On the other hand, speculators may take out several long positions. They believed that in this situation, the price of the future would be below the market price of the asset. The opposite effect should also hold true if there was a concern about rising prices and hedgers took out long positions and speculators took short positions. Here, the price of the future should be above the market price of the underlying asset.

Whether this is true or not has been subject to much debate. Regardless, the reason for this section was to briefly explain a few factors that can affect a contract's price outside of the demand for the underlying asset. This could have easily become a discussion on the various formulas that are used to value these contracts, but that is time consuming and verbose. This should suffice as an explanation towards slight effects in a contract's price, but it is by no means an explanation on determining the value a specific contract.

Types of Futures

Throughout this chapter, we have discussed only one type of future. Even though commodities are an important aspect of the futures market, there are several other types of futures that are traded. To be fair, you can apply everything in this chapter to these futures as well. The only difference being that the underlying assets on these futures are not physical commodities. Many of these futures instead have intangible assets underlying the futures.

Stock Futures: These futures are taken out on an individual stock in a company. Just like the previous futures, you can choose to buy or sell the stock within the future contract at a predetermined price.

Within these futures, the grade of the asset is not important as it all holds the same value.

Index Futures: The underlying asset in an index future is whatever index it is tracking. Examples of popular indexes include the S&P 500, Nasdaq, and Dow Jones. Similar to a commodity future, an investor can make or lose money depending on whether the price of the index rises or falls in value.

Currency Futures: Currency futures are very popular in the foreign exchange market. The underlying asset in a currency future is a specific country's currency. These futures are very popular among multi-national corporations. In fact, many companies will take multiple positions in various currencies in order to hedge their foreign exchange risk. Naturally, these futures are also popular among speculators. If the exchange rate of your home currency moves significantly, you stand to profit or suffer a loss on these futures.

Interest Rate Futures: An interest rate future is a little different from the other types of futures. The underlying asset in an interest-rate future is not an actual interest rate. Instead, the underlying asset is an interest paying asset. Using an interest rate future, an investor can secure the price of the interest paying asset on a future date. Typical underlying assets for this type of future are Treasury Bills, 30-year and 10-year Treasury Bonds, and Eurodollars. At the end of the contract, one party is required to buy the asset, and the other party must sell the asset. The factor to watch in these contracts is the current interest rate in the markets. As interest rates rise and fall it may make the underlying asset in your contract more or less valuable. Because these futures are used to hedge interest rate risk, they are very popular as a hedge in bond portfolios.

Hedging Using Futures in Practice

We already know that futures are excellent tools for hedging risk. We have not, however, discussed the situations hedgers often find themselves in, and the appropriate method of hedging in those situations. This section aims to clarify the way that hedging works in an actual situation.

To start, we must address the reality of a perfect hedge. These types of hedges are extremely rare. The reason for this rarity is the unfortunate fact that a company may buy or sell an asset on a date before or after a future expires. This leads to a disparity between the future expiration and the date when the company needs to hedge its risk. This disparity will be explored later in this section, but for now understand that a perfect hedge is difficult to obtain and not often observed in the real world.

Because a perfect hedge is oftentimes impossible to obtain, the goal should be to neutralize a risk as much as possible. Consider this, a company that deals in a certain commodity knows that for every 1 cent increase in the price of a commodity it will gain $15,000. Similarly, every 1 cent decrease in the price of the commodity will lead to a $15,000 loss. Clearly, there is an incentive to ensure that the risk is hedged. Ideally, the hedge would perfectly balance out the increase and decrease in price. Meaning that whether or not the price goes up or down, it does not affect the overall profit of the company because the hedge is offsetting any potential profits or losses as they occur. So, when and how should a company hedge its position?

There are times when a company already owns an asset. The company may be looking to sell the asset at a future date. In this situation, the company should use a short hedge. As the name implies, a short hedge involves a short position in a contract. By being on the selling side of a contract, the company is able to lock in the price that their asset will be sold for. A short hedge can also be used when an asset is not owned right now, but it will be owned at some point in the future. For example, a company that exports cars to Japan is expecting to receive yen in about 4 months. If the yen increases in value, the company will realize a gain when the yen is converted into the company's home currency. The opposite is also true, and the company may instead lose money when receiving the yen. By entering into a short hedge, the company can offset that gain or loss even though they do not currently own the asset.

The other type of hedge is a long hedge. A long hedge involves a long position in a contract. A long hedge is best used when a company knows that it will have to purchase an asset in the future. With a long hedge, the company can lock in the price of the asset now. Long hedges can also be used when a company is importing a product. A company may need to pay for something in a foreign currency. If the value of the company's home currency suddenly falls in comparison to the foreign currency, the company may lose significant amounts of money. While the opposite is also true, companies prefer to lock in their costs. With a long hedge, the company can offset any potential gain or loss in a changing exchange rate. In these situations, a long hedge is appropriate.

Regardless of which method of hedging a company uses, it is important to understand that a hedge can lead to a worse outcome for the company as a whole. For example, if an oil refinery is preparing to buy 20 million barrels of crude oil that it will refine into other products. The refinery will enter into a long hedge to lower its risk of a sudden rise in crude oil prices. If the price of crude oil instead falls, the gain that the refinery would have made on a lower price is offset by the loss on the future contract they entered into. Instead of gaining on lower input costs, the refinery has achieved a worse outcome than if they had not hedged. While this is unfortunate, many companies would still prefer to hedge their risk to a sudden increase in prices. A company must view hedging as a way to lower their risk, not as a way to make more profit.

One aspect that must be taken into account when creating a hedge is the difference between the market price of the asset when the company buys or sells it and the date when the future contract expires. As we stated earlier, the farther out the contract is from expiration, the greater the difference between the market and contract price. If an asset is bought or sold before or after the contract expires, there is a risk that the price of the future contract will not reflect the true price on the market. The farther out the expiration date, the more likely that the future price will differ from the market price. This risk is referred to as basis risk.

Basis risk can be calculated by subtracting the future price of the asset from the market price of the asset. If the basis risk increases, it is referred to as a strengthening of the basis. When the basis risk decreases, it is referred to as a weakening of the basis. Two factors affect the basis risk. The first being the underlying asset in the contract, and the second being the delivery month. We have already explained that basis risk increases as the time difference between the hedge expiration and the delivery month increases, but basis risk can also increase when the asset that needs to be hedged is different from the asset underlying the contract.

There is a practice known as cross hedging that companies will use when attempting to hedge their risks. When a company cross hedges, it increases the basis risk because of the first factor. Cross hedging occurs when a company enters into a futures contract for one asset that is different from the asset that they actually need to be hedged. A common example is that of an airline company. An airline needs to hedge its risk against rising jet fuel prices. Unfortunately for the airline, jet fuel futures do not exist. Instead, the airline enters into a futures contract for crude oil. This act of cross hedging helps to hedge the company's risk, but it increases their basis risk and ensures that they will not have a perfect hedge.

This is how hedging is used in practice and what companies are looking for when deciding what type of hedge to use. A perfect hedge is difficult to obtain, and companies need to understand that a hedge can lead to a worse outcome for the business. When a company decides to hedge, they must watch their basis risk. Basis risk increases the farther apart the hedge expiration and the contract expiration are and when the underlying asset being hedged is not the asset listed on the contract. Hedging is not an exciting topic, but it is important to understand due to the large role that it has in the futures markets.

Arbitrage

A discussion on the futures market would be incomplete without a brief glance at arbitrage. You may remember from the foreign exchange market that arbitrage occurs when an investor takes advantage of two or more markets to make a guaranteed profit on a trade. This occurs because the prices of the markets do not update instantaneously, and that delay in price changes can lead to an arbitrage opportunity that an investor can take advantage of. Even if just for a few seconds, arbitrage can give investors access to instant profit.

An arbitrage opportunity arises when the market price of the underlying asset falls out of line with the price of the contract. To take advantage of this difference, investors can use one of two strategies. The first strategy involves buying the underlying asset immediately and simultaneously shorting the future. The second strategy involves selling the underlying asset and then taking a long position in the future.

These strategies are most popular for index and stock futures because the underlying assets in those futures do not have any storage costs associated with them. These strategies can allow traders to make a guaranteed profit on a future because of the opposite positions that are taken when the market price and future price become unaligned. While the profit on arbitrage is typically small, with enough volume the profit made on arbitrage opportunities can be quite large. Usually, taking advantage of an arbitrage opportunity is never done by an actual person. Instead, computer programs are used to generate the trades before the arbitrage opportunity disappears.

Forwards vs. Futures

Okay, so maybe you've noticed by this point that the title of this chapter is "Forwards/Futures." Now, it seems that we have extensively covered futures, but what is a forward? The difference between a forward and a future is really not much. They are both used as a method of hedging against price fluctuations for specific assets and they serve the exact same purpose as a standard future contract.

So why the distinction? Forward contracts are different because it is a private agreement between two parties, and it is not traded on an exchange. It is still a contract, but the middleman, the exchange, has been cut out of the deal. Because it is a private agreement, it is more customizable, and the details of the contract remain private and are not publicly disclosed.

While the private nature of the contract and the potential reduction of fees might seem attractive, a forward contract does come with some downsides. Specifically, the contract is not backed by an exchange which guarantees delivery and acceptance of the asset. While difficult to break, there may come a situation where a party fails to deliver what they promised in the contract. The likelihood of a default on the contract is much higher in forwards when compared to futures. Which is why forward contracts should only be made between two parties that trust each other to deliver on their promises.

Lastly, a forward differs from a future in the way that they settle their accounts. In a future, the exchange settles the accounts on a daily basis and will call the investor if the maintenance margin is not met. In a forward, the contract is entirely settled once at the end of the contract.

While these are extremely similar contracts, the differences between them are significant enough to warrant an explanation. Of course, these contracts are not readily available to most investors, but they do play a role in the decisions of institutional investors and corporations, so they are worth understanding.

Futures are a complicated asset to understand, and many people have difficulty grasping it immediately. This market is especially valuable because of the important role that it plays in helping to hedge risk. Without this market, many corporations would be unable to lower some of the risks that they take on every day. This market has existed for hundreds of years, and it will continue to exist as long as these needs arise.

7.

Options Market

Options can be a complicated and tricky subject to cover. Fortunately, much of the information to understand options has already been covered. An option is very similar to a future. Options are still derivatives that have an underlying asset and a set expiration date. The key difference between them is in the name. In a future contract, the buyer or seller of the contract is **required** to buy or sell the underlying asset on the contracted date. In an option, the investor is given the **right** to buy or sell the underlying asset on the expiration date. So, an option contract gives you the option to buy or sell the asset, not just the requirement to do so.

Options can be purchased in two distinct places. The first are formal exchanges. This is where the vast majority of option contracts are purchased. An **exchange-traded option** is a standardized contract that is traded on an exchange. The exchange has standardized the contracts to have similar strike prices, quantities, and expiration dates. Because more investors are attracted to these exchanges, it leads to greater liquidity for these types of options. The exchanges also guarantee that the contracts can be exercised and will not default. The second way to purchase an option is in the over-the-counter market. In the OTC market, there is no formal exchange. All transactions occur directly between buyers and sellers. While this may lead to a higher risk of default, an **OTC option** is very customizable and can fill the specific needs of an investor. The parties in an OTC option get to decide what the terms are and can best achieve their desired positions down to the most intricate detail. Additionally, the options are private, and the details of the contract do not need to be publicly disclosed. Default risk is higher with these options, but many investors believe the benefits of the OTC market outweigh the potential costs. Because exchange-traded options are more common and the details of these contracts are publicly disclosed, the options that are discussed in this book will be exchange-traded options unless specified otherwise.

There are two classes of options that investors can buy and sell. The first option is a European option. European options can only be exercised on the maturity date. This means that you cannot buy or sell the underlying asset until the expiration date is reached. The second class of option are American options. An American option can be exercised at any time during its life. With an

American option you can buy or sell the underlying asset whenever you want. Of course, even if you cannot buy or sell the underlying asset at any time in a European option, you can still sell the contract to another investor. For the purposes of this book, we will assume that all options discussed are American options unless explicitly stated otherwise. Additionally, it will be assumed that the underlying asset in these option contracts are stocks, not a commodity or currency.

If an option gives investors the choice to buy or sell the underlying asset and not the legal obligation to do so, why doesn't everyone just use options instead of futures? There are several reasons why a future is more advantageous than an option. Those reasons include greater liquidity, relatively unchanged trading costs, and easier to understand pricing information. The primary reason, however, is because investors must pay an **option premium** up front in order to create the option contract. Remember that options have the advantage of choice. Investors pay for that choice in the option premium. If the option premium is too high, investors may prefer futures to lower their trading costs.

Within the option market, there are two types of options that investors can purchase. These options are referred to as calls and puts. A **call option** gives an investor the right, but not the obligation, to **purchase** the underlying asset at the set price in the contract. A **put option** gives the investor the right, but not the obligation, to **sell** the underlying asset at the set price in the contract. In the options market, the set price in the contract is the strike price. So, if you buy a call option with a strike price of $47 and for 100 units, it gives you the right to purchase 100 units at $47/unit. This can be very profitable if the current market price of the stock is higher than the rate that you paid when the contract expires.

Now that we understand the basics of what an option is, we can move onto what makes these assets so important in the financial world.

Option Terminology	
Units	The number of a specific asset that investors can choose to purchase or sell (depending on the contract) when the contract expires.
Option Premium	The price investors pay to create the option contract. This is the "cost" of the option.
Strike Price	The specified price that investors are allowed to purchase or sell shares at.
Expiration Date	The date on which the contract expires, and when the investor is allowed to buy or sell the underlying asset.

Option Positions

In the futures market, there are only two possible choices available to investors. An investor is only able to buy or sell a contract. In the options market, it is more complicated because investors actually have four positions that they can take. Before explaining these positions, it is important to understand that the definitions of certain terms change in the options market. In other markets, if you were long in an investment you believed the asset would increase in value. If you were short in an investment, you believed the asset would decrease in value. Now, we need to reprogram ourselves to understand that a long and short position are different when referring to options. Below, are the four positions that investors can take in an option.

1. Buy a call
2. Sell a call
3. Buy a put
4. Sell a put

As you can see, investors are not only able to buy calls and puts, but they can also sell calls and puts to other investors. When an investor sells an option, they are agreeing to buy or sell the asset from the investor that is purchasing the option. Selling an option contract to another investor is also referred to as "writing" a contract. If an investor writes a call contract to another investor, they are agreeing to sell the other investor the underlying asset at the strike price. If an investor writes a put contract, they are agreeing to buy the underlying asset from the other investor at the strike price.

Why would an investor want to write a contract? Remember the option premium that the buyer of an option contract pays? That option premium is paid to the person that writes the option contract. This means that the seller of an option has an up-front profit that they charge the buyer, but potential liability later on. The buyer of an option has an up-front cost, but potential profit later on.

Because of this difference between those that are buying and writing the contracts, we change the way that we refer to these positions as well. If you say that someone is long on an option, it means that they are buying the option. If you instead say that someone is short on an option, it means that they are writing the option. Remember this, because being long or short in a contract just refers to whether you bought or sold the option. It does not indicate whether you think the underlying asset will go up or down.

Now that we understand the distinction between long and short positions, we can rewrite the four option positions as follows.

1. Long call
2. Short call
3. Long put
4. Short put

If the positions in the options market allow investors to go long on both calls and puts, what methods should investors use? In reality, the choices that investors make is dependent on what they believe the future will hold. For example, investors that believe an asset will increase in value may consider a long call or a short put. If they believe that an asset will decrease in value, they may instead be interested in a short call or a long put.

Another factor that investors need to consider is the amount of volatility that a specific asset is experiencing. The more volatile the market, the more potential for value a long position may have. If a contract expires and the underlying asset's price is much lower or higher than the strike price, depending on which side of the contract you are on, the contract may be worth a significant amount of money. Instead, the market may be very stable and not moving very much. In this situation, writing a call or put is more beneficial. If the underlying asset's price does not move much, then the asset may never change farther than the option premium. In which case, the money will be made by the writers. So, future expectations and the expected volatility of the underlying asset will affect the strategies undertaken by investors.

Positions to take depending on the investor's sentiment	
Investor believes that the asset price will increase	1. Long call 2. Short put
Investor believes that the asset price will decrease	1. Short call 2. Long put

Leverage

If you remember in Chapter 6, we discussed a concept known as margin. In futures, margin was required in order to enter into a contract. In the options market, margin is not a requirement. Even though certain option positions require margin, the market itself does not require the use of margin. Instead, leverage is the focus of study in the options market.

Leverage is the ability to take a position in larger amounts of an asset than you would normally be allowed to. You may be thinking that this sounds very similar to margin. In the sense of leverage and margin allowing investors to take larger than normal positions, they have the same effect. What is different is the way that they go about it. In margin, the investor is using borrowed money to enter a position. Instead, options are inherently leveraged financial instruments.

How are options inherently leveraged? The leverage comes from the contract's details. In a standard stock option, the underlying asset is 100 shares of the company stock that the investor is taking a position in. The investor is expected to pay the option premium up-front and not much else. This can allow an investor to take positions far larger than simply using a margin account to just purchase the stock. Is this still confusing? Here is an example of an investor named Kevin and a long call option contract.

Kevin: $750

Call option: ABC Company
Number of shares per contract: 100
Strike Price: $25
Current market price per share of ABC Company: $25
Option Premium: $1.50

To keep things simple for this example, the strike price and current market price are the same price. It should be noted that there is usually a difference between those parts on an option. Regardless, the important part of this example is the $1.50 option premium. This premium is paid for each unit of the underlying asset in the contract. Here, one contract would cost 100 times $1.50. That is a total of $150 per contract. With this information, our example investor has a decision to make.

Kevin has two choices that he can make. First, he can just buy the underlying stock. With $750, Kevin can afford to purchase 30 shares. Those 30 shares are his and he owns them. Kevin's other choice is to instead use that money to buy long call options. With $750 he can purchase 5 option contracts at $150 per contract. With 5 contracts, Kevin now has a stake in 500 shares of ABC Company. By taking the second choice, Kevin can control a little over 16 times more shares than he normally could through the stock market!

This should not be taken as all good news. Leverage is a dangerous double-edged sword. Yes, it can make an investor a lot of money, but it can also lead an investor to lose his entire investment if the options expire worthless. If an investor had instead just purchased the shares in the stock market, they might lose money, but the stock will likely still retain some value. Leverage is a powerful tool, but an investor's risk should be assessed before taking any position.

Another problem with leverage and options is the way in which the price of an option and the underlying asset move. Often times a stock option will only move a fraction of the price change on the underlying asset. The amount that a contract moves is based on the delta value. I will not bore you with the math, but a delta is a measure of how much the price of the contract changes in relation to its underlying asset. If a contract has a delta of 0.3, it means that for every $1 change in the underlying asset, the contract will only move $0.30. Delta is especially important for hedgers looking to perfectly hedge their risk.

Because delta affects the overall leverage in a position, it is important for an investor to understand how much leverage they have taken on. The larger the leverage becomes, the greater the potential gain or loss becomes on the position. Even though margin and leverage accomplish the same goal, leverage can be used to take far larger positions that investors would have otherwise been unable to access. Because options are such leveraged financial instruments, investors are not allowed to use margin accounts when purchasing options. Traders who write options, however, must maintain a margin account to ensure proper transfer of funds.

Types of Options Traders

Similar to other markets, we have the same types of traders in the options market. Specifically, hedgers, speculators, and arbitrageurs exist in this market.

Hedgers: Options are a popular tool to hedge against a change in value. The hedgers in the option market tend to be hedging large stock portfolios instead of a specific commodity. Because of the leverage offered by options, hedgers can put up a small amount of capital to hedge an extremely large position. Additionally, options are offered on individual stocks more often than futures. This has made them extremely popular among investors looking to hedge a specific position.

Speculators: If there is one word to describe speculators, it would have to be volatility. Speculators thrive in volatility. If a stock is rising rapidly, option owners are either losing their positions or making massive returns. Because there is so much leverage involved in options, speculators can gamble on more stocks than they would be able to purchase on their own. As a result, the potential returns are great, but the risk is enormous. Plenty of speculators have watched their options expire worthless and lost their entire position in the process.

Arbitrageurs: Arbitrage is the exact same here as it is in other markets. Arbitrageurs take advantage of the pricing differences in two or more markets to generate a guaranteed profit. In options, a pricing difference occurs between an identical call and put. Two main strategies are used by arbitrageurs when this price difference occurs. The first strategy involves buying the underlying stock on the contract and simultaneously buying the identical put and selling the call. The second strategy occurs by shorting the underlying stock and selling a put and buying a call. The arbitrage profit in these situations is made up of the difference in price of the two contracts in relation to the underlying asset. These opportunities are extremely rare, and they only last for a few seconds to a few minutes at a time. The average investor will not be able to take advantage of these opportunities when they arise.

Reading Option Price Quotes

Similar to other markets, options have an entirely different language that they use to communicate prices. When starting to read these quotes, it can feel overwhelming and confusing. By dissecting and analyzing each section on a quote, we can unravel the complicated aspects of learning this new language.

To start, we need to look at an **option chain**. An option chain is what brokers use to display option quotes row by row. On the next page is an option chain for Carnival Cruise Line (CCL). If you would like to look at other option chains for different companies, this chart was obtained from Yahoo Finance.

CCL210618C00023500	2021-06-01 11:36AM EDT	23.50	7.03	5.80	5.95	0.00	-	4	4	208.59%
CCL210618C00024000	2021-06-15 2:40PM EDT	24.00	4.61	5.30	5.40	0.00	-	50	49	184.38%
CCL210618C00024500	2021-06-15 10:21AM EDT	24.50	4.40	4.80	4.95	0.00	-	4	7	176.95%
CCL210618C00025000	2021-06-17 9:52AM EDT	25.00	4.30	4.30	4.40	0.00	-	15	3,889	153.91%
CCL210618C00025500	2021-06-16 12:36PM EDT	25.50	3.55	3.80	3.95	0.00	-	13	783	145.70%
CCL210618C00026000	2021-06-16 3:45PM EDT	26.00	3.35	3.30	3.40	+0.05	+1.52%	11	1,327	123.44%
CCL210618C00026500	2021-06-17 9:42AM EDT	26.50	2.84	2.82	2.86	-0.04	-1.39%	14	259	105.47%
CCL210618C00027000	2021-06-17 9:36AM EDT	27.00	2.62	2.32	2.37	+0.25	+10.55%	33	414	91.80%
CCL210618C00027500	2021-06-17 9:50AM EDT	27.50	1.92	1.85	1.90	+0.06	+3.23%	6	12,876	82.42%
CCL210618C00028000	2021-06-17 9:54AM EDT	28.00	1.42	1.35	1.40	+0.02	+1.43%	16	1,018	65.63%
CCL210618C00028500	2021-06-17 9:58AM EDT	28.50	0.95	0.93	0.97	-0.01	-1.04%	109	1,672	58.98%
CCL210618C00029000	2021-06-17 9:43AM EDT	29.00	0.54	0.53	0.55	-0.03	-5.26%	682	3,881	49.41%
CCL210618C00029500	2021-06-17 9:58AM EDT	29.50	0.27	0.24	0.27	-0.05	-15.62%	700	3,460	44.92%
CCL210618C00030000	2021-06-17 9:57AM EDT	30.00	0.12	0.11	0.12	-0.06	-33.33%	3,503	31,729	44.53%
CCL210618C00030500	2021-06-17 9:54AM EDT	30.50	0.06	0.05	0.07	-0.04	-40.00%	132	4,368	50.39%
CCL210618C00031000	2021-06-17 9:54AM EDT	31.00	0.04	0.03	0.05	-0.02	-33.33%	136	9,518	54.69%
CCL210618C00031500	2021-06-17 9:52AM EDT	31.50	0.03	0.03	0.04	-0.01	-25.00%	17	3,973	64.06%
CCL210618C00032000	2021-06-17 9:49AM EDT	32.00	0.03	0.02	0.03	0.00	-	75	3,566	69.53%
CCL210618C00032500	2021-06-17 9:51AM EDT	32.50	0.02	0.01	0.02	-0.01	-33.33%	139	8,032	71.88%

To be fair, this is not all of the options that were available for this stock at the time of this writing. In fact, this was just a portion of the available options trading for this asset. All of the options that are listed in this photo are calls. If you would have continued to scroll down, you would have also found quotes for the available put options at that time.

The most obvious thing that you may have noticed from this picture is the difference in shading between these calls. The calls that are shaded are “in the money.” The non-shaded calls are “out of the money.” We will cover the differences between those later, but for now it is enough to know what that means.

The most complicated part of this option chain is the first column. To keep things simple, let’s look at the first row and first column. It reads CCL210618C00023500. That first column gives us more information about the option than the rest of the chart. CCL is the ticker symbol for the underlying asset. In this case, CCL is referencing Carnival Cruise Line as the underlying asset. "210618" references the expiration date for this option. In this case, the option is expiring on June 18, 2021.

If you pay attention to detail, you may have noticed the letter that breaks up the two numbers in the option quote. That letter is C. In this case, that C is referencing that this is a call option. In a put option, the letter would be P. The second group of numbers is "00023500." Those numbers are letting the investor know what the strike price is for the option. The strike price for this option is $23.50. With just the first column, an educated investor can glean very important information about the option contract in an extremely concise manner.

Moving on from the first column, we have the second column that references the last time that this option contract was traded. Investors often confuse the second column with the expiration date for the contract. In reality, the second column is allowing investors to see the last time a trade was placed for this specific contract, not the date on which the contract will expire. The third column is the strike price written again in simpler terms. Because these are calls, the strike price is the price at which the investor has the right to purchase CCL.

The fourth column is the last price that the contract was traded for. This is the last recorded price of the option contract. This may not reflect the current market value of the option, but it is a useful tool to see the last settled price.

The fifth and sixth columns are the bid and ask prices, respectively. The bid price is the price that a buyer wants to buy the option at, and the ask price is the price that the seller wants to sell the contract at. Whatever the price settles on is the premium that is paid for that contract. Each of these prices are for contracts with 100 shares of stock. So, the real price of the option would be the bid or ask price multiplied by 100.

The seventh and eighth columns also go together, and they are the change and percentage change respectively. If the price of the option changes from the previous day's closing, it is reflected in the seventh column. The magnitude of that change is then reflected in the eighth column. Large or small changes in price are reflected in the eighth column, and the actual number of that change is in the seventh column.

The ninth column is the volume on the specific contract. The volume on a contract is the number of contracts that were traded on the current day. While this shows how much a contract is moving on a specific day, it is not an indicator of how often the contract is being traded on a regular basis.

The tenth column is the open interest on a contract. Open interest is considered to be a better measure of the overall liquidity of a contract than volume. Open interest refers to the number of contracts that are currently outstanding. If a contract is outstanding, it means that the contracts have not yet been closed, exercised, or expired. Effectively, open interest allows investors to know how many active contracts are still out in the market. These active contracts have been traded, but they have not been liquidated by the investor through an offsetting trade or simply exercised. Open interest allows investors to know how liquid their contract is. The larger the open interest, the larger the secondary market for that specific option is. As the secondary market grows larger, it is easier for an investor to liquidate their position.

Lastly, we have the eleventh column. The eleventh column is the implied volatility of the option. The implied volatility is used to show investors how volatile the underlying asset on an option contract may be. Volatility is just market sentiment on how much the price of the stock will swing in either direction. It does not imply which direction it will go.

After reading through this section, you should feel comfortable reading option chains and understanding what everything means. You can always refer to this book if you feel there is something that you have forgotten or wish to better understand.

What Affects an Option's Price?

Now that we have a better understanding of options, we can focus on the factors that influence an option's price. In total, there are six factors that affect an option's price. In this section, each of those factors is explored and explained. We are also assuming that the underlying asset is a stock.

Underlying Asset Price: This is probably the most important factor as it relates to options. In the case of a stock option, the price of the stock will have the greatest impact on the price of the option. Assuming that the investor took a long position, a long call becomes more valuable as the stock price rises, and a long put becomes more valuable as the stock price falls. This is usually the primary cause of an increase or decrease in an option's price.

Strike Price: A contract's strike price is an important consideration for an investor. The strike price affects how quickly an option contract can become profitable. If an option's strike price is close to the current stock price, a slight change in the underlying asset's price may allow an option to become profitable. Of course, this all depends on the type of contract that you have. In a long call, when the stock price is higher than the strike price, the option's price will increase. The same price on a long put will create an option that trades at a very low price. If nothing changes, the put option may expire worthless. Depending on the contract, a higher or lower strike price may lead to a more expensive or cheaper contract. In a long call, is a lower or higher strike price more valuable? Remember, the lower the strike price the cheaper that an investor is given the choice to purchase the underlying asset when the option expires. Therefore, a lower strike price would be more valuable in a long call. This additional value is reflected by having a contract that is more expensive than the contract with a higher strike price. This is assuming that we have two contracts that are the same with different strike prices.

Time to Expiration: This is a strange phenomenon in the options market. Typically, both call and put options become more valuable the farther they are from expiring. This is because the investor has more time to exercise their option. This additional time is associated with a higher cost for the investor. As an option comes closer to expiration, the value of the option will start to decline. This decline in value is referred to as time decay.

Volatility: Volatility is very important to both buyers and writers of options. Volatility is how uncertain the market feels about future price movements. A stock is more stable as volatility decreases. As volatility increases, the price swings of the stock also increase. Higher volatility leads to higher option premiums as the risk to writers increases. As volatility lowers, writers compete with each other to offer the cheapest option contracts while still making a profit.

Risk-Free Interest Rate: The risk-free interest rate was an important factor in the bond market, but it influences the options market as well. Because the U.S. Government sets the risk-free rate, it influences the stock and bond market as a whole. As the risk-free rate rises, it causes interest rates in the economy to also increase. This leads to higher returns on "safe" assets like bonds. When this occurs, money flows out of the stock market and into the bond market. This will affect an option whose underlying asset is a stock. When interest rates rise, it causes stock prices to fall. This causes the prices of call options to fall, and the prices of put options to rise. The opposite effect will also occur. As interest rates fall, it causes stock prices to rise. This increases the value of call options and decreases the value of put options. The risk-free interest rate is an indirect factor in the options market, but it influences the market regardless.

Dividends: Remember dividends? If the underlying asset on an option contract is a stock, it would make sense that the stock may issue dividends, right? Well, dividends affect the stock price by reducing the stock price when a dividend is declared. Typically, a company's stock will decrease by about the same amount as the dividend that was declared. So, a larger dividend would lead to a larger decrease in the stock price. Consider a stock option that has a dividend declared during the life of the option. Because dividends decrease the stock price, a call option would be negatively affected, and a put option would be positively affected.

Valuing Options

Now that we understand the various factors that affect an option's price, we can learn about option pricing theory. In option pricing theory, formulas and simulations are used in order to determine what the value of an option should be. Using these methods, an investor should be able to estimate an option's fair value.

There are several models that have been developed over the years that are used in these estimations. The most commonly used model includes Black-Scholes, binomial option pricing, and Monte-Carlo simulations. These models attempt to calculate the probability that an option will be profitable at the time that it expires. By inputting several factors, these formulas can be used as estimations of value.

Unfortunately, many of these models have significant flaws. While these models are excellent for teaching beginners how options are priced, they regularly fail in real-world application. Of course, they do work sometimes. So, calling them complete failures would be an insult to the work that was put into developing and curating these models.

The first model, and most taught model, is the Black-Scholes-Merton Pricing model. This model was developed by Fischer Black, Myron Scholes, and Robert Merton. Yes, they really did name their model after themselves. I refuse to bore you with the details of the model, but the model is worth mentioning for its wide-spread use. I will not get into explaining the formula details, but here is the formula for European calls and puts. (c = call, p = put)

$$c = S_0 N(d_1) - Ke^{-rt} N(d_2)$$

$$p = Ke^{-rt} N(-d_2) - S_0 N(-d_1)$$

where

$$d_1 = \frac{\ln(S_0/K) + (r + (\sigma^2/2))T}{\sigma \sqrt{T}}$$

$$d_2 = = \frac{\ln(S_0/K) + (r - (\sigma^2/2))T}{\sigma \sqrt{T}} = d_1 - \sigma \sqrt{T}$$

It is a rather complex model which warrants a mention as one of the most accurate methods we have today to predict the prices of options. In order to develop their model, they had to make several assumptions. Because their assumptions were so specific, many options in the real world do not fit the specifications that they set. Below are the assumptions that the Black-Scholes-Merton model requires.

1. Stock price behavior aligns itself according to a lognormal model where μ and σ are constant. A lognormal distribution is used instead of a normal distribution for two reasons. The first being that a lognormal distribution can only be positive. This is different from a normal distribution which can be both positive and negative. Secondly, a lognormal distribution has a special property where the natural logarithm in the model is normally distributed. If we take the natural log of a stock price, then the stock price will be assumed to be normally distributed. This is why in the above formula we have "$\ln S_0$." In this model, the assumption is a lognormal distribution, not a normal distribution. Do not be too concerned about understanding this. It is not necessary for an understanding of the options markets as a whole.
2. Transaction costs and taxes are non-existent. Securities are perfectly divisible.
3. There are no dividends on the stock for the life of the contract.
4. Arbitrage opportunities do not exist, and nobody can take advantage of a pricing error in the markets.
5. Trading is continuous
6. Investors can borrow at the risk-free rate of interest.

7. The risk-free rate is constant and will not change in the near future.

As you can see, many of these assumptions cannot be applied in the real world. This model was also developed for European options, not American options. This model also takes into account the expected return and volatility for an asset. Both of which are difficult variables to obtain a concrete number for. Even with the numbers in the formula, many assumptions have to be made. I will not be writing about the different variables in this formula, but it is important to recognize this model as an extremely prominent model that is still used to this day. Even if it is difficult to use and relies on a lot of assumptions.

The second model used to price options is the binomial option pricing model. This model is also referred to as binomial trees because of the way that the model looks. This model was developed a few years after the Black-Scholes-Merton model. The binomial model shows the different paths that a stock price may follow over the life of an option.

Here is an example of a binomial tree. Pretend that an investor has a stock that costs $50 and they know that in 6 months the stock will be worth $60 or $40. The binomial tree will look like this.

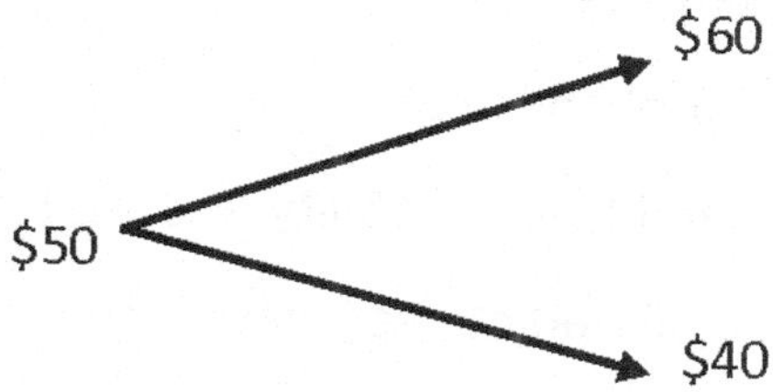

Using this, an investor could theoretically construct a portfolio that matches the risk-free rate of return. They do this by obtaining the delta Δ and constructing a portfolio around that. Don't worry, I will not be covering that. I understand that this section may be difficult to read through due to the nature of option pricing theory. I am avoiding much of the actual math that goes into these calculations because I understand that it is not an interesting part of the options market.

While this was a simple example, you may have noticed something about this example that seems strange. Specifically, how did the investor know what the stock price would be in 6 months? In the real world, nobody knows what the stock price is going to do. Because nobody knows which way the stock will go, potential option investors do not spend all of their time constructing binomial trees for every possibility. Instead, they have computers do it. The computers do not look at only two potential outcomes. Instead, the computer develops models based on the probabilities that the investor enters into the system.

Those probabilities are assumed by the investor. In the example above, we assumed a 50/50 probability of the two potential future events. In reality, what if the probability was 70/30 or 15/85? That probability has to be assumed by the investor and created based on what they think will occur. Lastly, the binomial tree that we looked at only had 1 time step. A computer will often develop models that have 30 or more time steps before the contract will expire. This can lead to billions of possible stock price paths that a computer will develop and present to an investor. Like the rest of these models, the binomial option pricing model is reliant on assumptions of the overall market, and what the investor believes will occur.

Lastly, we have the Monte-Carlo simulation model. This model is interesting because its applications have been extended to various fields of study. A Monte-Carlo simulation is often run for situations in which a future outcome cannot be easily predicted. These situations often have random variables that make future predictions difficult to determine.

In a Monte Carlo simulation, one unknown variable is isolated. That variable is then assigned a random value by the simulation. Then the simulation runs the model and obtains the result with the random value. The simulation proceeds to do this and assigns a random value to the isolated variable every single time. After running the model hundreds if not thousands of times, the results are averaged together to provide an estimate of what may happen. While a crude model, it works fairly well for many industries.

In stock options, the isolated variable is the stock price. These simulations assume a perfectly efficient market, and it ignores many of the outside factors that have anything to do with price movements. Once the model has been run and the results collected, a normal distribution can be assumed, and the future price movement should fall within 2 or 3 standard deviations of the simulation.

These simulations are fun, but like every other model on this list, it has major flaws and ultimately can never perfectly predict the market. This is an oversimplified section. For brevity, much of the finer details of these models has been left out. While it may benefit the reader to understand what investors use to determine an option's fair value, it ultimately does not assist in understanding the options market as a whole. That is why these models have been mentioned, but little attention will be paid to them from here on out.

Option Market Terminology

We have already covered many of the common terms that are used in the options market. Specifically, we have already covered the common terms used in an options contract. Terms like units, option premium, strike price, expiration date, and underlying asset have already been covered. Additionally, the terms used to describe an option position have already been covered as well. There are a few terms that we have not yet covered, and we are going to be going over those here.

To start, there are three major terms that are used to describe what an option is worth. With these terms, investors know if a contract currently holds intrinsic value or not.

The first term is “in the money.” This term was briefly mentioned in the section about reading price quotes. When an option is referred to as in the money, it means that the current stock price and the strike price on the option favors the option holder. If the option is a call, then the current stock price is higher than the strike price on the option. If the option is a put, then the current stock price is lower than the strike price. In both of these situations, the option holds some form of intrinsic value and should be worth something if it expired.

The second term is “out of the money.” When an option is out of the money, it means that the current stock price and strike price on the option does not favor the option holder. An out of the money option has no financial benefit to being exercised. If you are holding an option like this, it would be less expensive to simply purchase the shares directly on the open market, or more lucrative to sell your shares at the current market rate. An out of the money option occurs in two situations. If the option is a call, then the current stock price is lower than the strike price. If the option is a put, then the current stock price is higher than the strike price.

The last major term used in describing the worth of an option is "at the money." If an option is at the money, the stock price is equal to or very close to the strike price. These contracts do not hold any real value because an investor can just purchase the shares on the open market for the current price. Instead, the investor paid for a contract that is no different than the current price.

There is one last broad term that is used in the option market. This term is used by risk managers to describe the different variables that they analyze when choosing to invest in an asset. These various risks are measured by the "Greeks." Many of the variables in the Greeks are actual Greek symbols. Unfortunately, there is no perfect variable that can analyze every different risk factor and numerically categorize it. As a result, risk managers rely on several of these Greeks to decide whether to enter into an option position.

An extensive analysis could be made of the Greeks, but I have found that the study of the Greeks is best left to people who will actually use it. I will not be delving into each variable and what it means. Keep in mind that these symbols are heavily math focused, and it would require another separate chapter to explain. Because knowledge of these symbols and what they represent would not aid in understanding the options market, they have been left out to keep things simple. Below is a brief list of the common Greeks and their symbols. This is not a comprehensive list, and there are several other Greeks that have been left out because they are not used as often as the ones below.

Delta (Δ)

Theta (Θ)

Gamma (Γ)

Rho (p)

Vega (V)

Potential Profit

Now that we have gotten through the basics of the options market, we can learn about actually making money. The best way to learn about making money in the options market is to analyze the potential profit and loss in each position. This section will cover the four option positions and the situations in which an investor turns a profit when the option expires.

Long Call: In a long call, an investor is purchasing a call option. When a call option is purchased, the option holder wants the stock price to rise. In order for the investor to turn a profit in their position, the stock price must surpass the combined stock price and option premium. Here is an example. A call option is purchased with a strike price of $120. The option premium that the investor pays is $7. In order to make money on the long call, the investor needs the stock price to rise above $127. If the price rises to $126 and expires, the option will be in the money, but the investor will have lost money on the position. Of course, the opposite effect could also occur. If the stock price dropped to $119, the options would be worthless, and the investor would lose his entire investment. The potential profit on this investment is considered to be unlimited as the stock price can continue to rise without restriction.

Short Call: In a short call, an option writer is selling a call option. When the call option is sold, the option writer collects the option premium as payment. The option writer wants the stock price to remain stable and not move or for the price to drop. Here is an example. A call option is sold with a strike price of $50. The option premium that the writer collects is $4. In order for the option writer to make money on the short call, the stock must not rise above $54. If the price rises to $57, the writer may have to sell the stocks for $50 to the option holder. Not only would the contract be out of the money, but the writer would lose $3 for each share on the contract. If the share price only rose to $52, then the writer would stand to profit $2 for writing the call. If the stock price falls below $50, then the writer will profit the total option premium. The maximum potential profit for this position would be the option premium, but the potential loss is unlimited.

Long Put: In a long put, the investor is purchasing a put option. When a put option is purchased, the investor wants the stock price to fall. In order for the investor to make a profit, the stock price must fall below the strike price subtracted from the option premium. Here is an example. A put option is purchased with a strike price of $20. The option premium that the investor pays is $5. In order to make money on the long put, the investor needs the stock price to fall below $15. If the stock price falls to $18, the option will be in the money, but the position will suffer a loss. If the stock price rises above $20, the entire contract is worthless. The potential loss on a long put is the total amount of money used to purchase put options. If the contract expires worthless, the investor will lose their entire position, but will not be required to sell the stock at the contracted price. So, the maximum potential loss on a long put is the position going to $0. The maximum potential profit on a long put occurs if the stock price goes to $0. The maximum potential profit on a long put would be the strike price subtracted from the option premium.

Short Put: In a short put, an option writer is selling a put option. When the put option is sold, the option writer collects the option premium. The option writer wants the stock price to rise or to remain relatively stable. Here is an example. A put option is sold with a strike price of $300. The option premium that the writer collects is $20. In order to make a profit, the stock price must not fall below $280. If the stock price stays above $300, the writer will get to keep the entire option premium. If the stock price falls to $290, the position will still be profitable, and the writer will still make $10. The maximum potential profit for this position would be the option premium. The maximum potential loss would occur if the stock price fell to $0. In which case, the maximum potential loss would be the strike price subtracted from the option premium.

Option Position	Favorable Stock Movement	Potential Profit	Potential Loss
Long Call	stock price rises	unlimited	entire position
Short Call	stock price falls	option premium	unlimited
Long Put	stock price falls	strike price – option premium	entire position
Short Put	stock price rises	option premium	strike price – option premium

What happens if a stock split occurs before expiration?

If you remember from Chapter 2, we discussed stock splits. A stock split is a corporate action that splits the price of a share by a set ratio, and it increases the number of shares in circulation by the same ratio. For example, a 2/1 or 3/1 stock split is fairly common for many companies.

What happens to options when this occurs? After all, the contract has a strike price that the stock is contracted to be traded at. A stock split would be great news for put holders and decimate call holders. In these situations, the option will adjust the terms of the contract to reflect the stock split.

Take a call option with a $100 strike price for 100 shares of ABC Company. If a 2/1 stock split occurred, the option would adjust to reflect the new changes. The strike price will change to $50 and the number of shares on the contract would increase to 200.

The opposite affect would occur in a reverse stock split. Assuming a 1/2 reverse stock split, the strike price will change to $200 and the number of shares will decrease to 50.

Other Types of Underlying Assets

Throughout this chapter, the assumption has been that the underlying asset on these option contracts is a company's stock.

While stock options are a very common type of option, there are other underlying assets that can be used in an option contract. This section is dedicated to addressing those other underlying assets.

Foreign Currency: While many use futures to hedge against foreign exchange risk, it is possible to find options that use a foreign currency as its underlying asset. There are a couple major exchanges that offer these options in the United States. The options are quoted in U.S. dollars per unit of the underlying foreign currency. Additionally, the option premiums are paid in U.S dollars, and when the contract settles, the payment is received in U.S dollars. This allows for an easy calculation for profit and loss in a position because everything is in U.S. dollars. The underlying foreign currency dictates how many units are in each contract. For example, the British pound may have a contract for 10,000 units. The Japanese yen, however, may have a contract for 1,000,000 units. It ultimately depends on the exchange and the contract size they are offering.

Indexes: Sometimes, an investor may not be looking to take a bet in an individual stock. Perhaps they need to take a position in the market as a whole or a specific segment of the market. With an index option, the investor can enter into a contract where a specific index is listed as the underlying asset. These contracts typically trade with contract sizes of 100. This means that one contract is for 100 indexes. When the contract settles, the settlement is in cash. That way the entire portfolio that is underlying the index is not delivered. For example, an option that has the S&P 500 index as an underlying asset. The 500 largest American company's stocks are not delivered to the investor. The price of the index at expiration is what the contract is settled for.

Bonds: A bond option is quite simple. It is very similar to stock options and there is not much difference between them. While stocks are more volatile, bonds tend to be safer assets. This might lead to the underlying asset not moving in price very much throughout the life of the contract. Because volatility decreases, it may lead to a decrease in the option premium charged on these options.

Futures: In the previous chapter, we covered the role of exchanges that create the contracts that investors purchase. When an exchange trades a specific future contract, they often offer options on the same contract. This means that the price of the future contract becomes the underlying asset. This is significant because the underlying asset is not the commodity that is being traded on the future. The underlying asset in a futures option is the price of the future contract, not the underlying asset on the future. When the option is exercised, the investor obtains the future contract. If a long call futures option is exercised, the investor is given a long future contract. If a long put futures option is exercised, the investor is given a short future contract. It is important that investors understand that the underlying asset in a futures option contract is the future contract, not the underlying asset that is listed on the future.

Options: An options contract can actually have another options contract as its underlying asset. This type of option is not widely popular and is not offered in most situations. The majority of investors cannot purchase these types of options as they are considered to be exotic and often exclusive to high end investors.

Swap: A swap is a financial tool that this book has not yet discussed. While an entire chapter could be dedicated to swaps and what they are used for, it is an exclusive market that the vast majority of individuals will never have to encounter. So, it will be briefly covered here. Keep in mind that this is a simplified version of a swap. It is by no means a comprehensive explanation on every aspect of a swap contract. As the name implies, a swap is a contract that two parties enter in order to swap something. In a swap, two parties come together and agree to swap cash flows for a set period of time. This is often used by a company that would like to change the type of interest that they are paying on a loan. For example, one company may have a loan with a fixed interest rate and another company has a loan with a variable interest rate. With a swap, the two companies can basically swap their interest rates. A bank will often oversee the transaction and ensure that neither party defaults. Obviously, there is more that goes into this, but this is basically how swaps work. In a swap option or swaption, an investor is given the right to enter into a swap contract at a specified future date.

Other Types of Options

There are several special types of options that are worth mentioning. Some of these options are not available to the general public, but they are considered options because of the way they work.

Warrant: No, this is not a warrant for someone's arrest. A stock warrant gives the holder the right to buy or sell a company's stock at a predetermined date and price. This sounds just like an option. Why the distinction? A warrant is issued directly by the company on the contract. In a stock option, the option is sold by another investor. The primary difference between these financial instruments is the issuer. When a warrant is exercised, the investor receives new shares. The shares are not on the secondary market.

Instead, the company issues new shares to the investor, and the company receives payment for the shares that are given to the investor.

Employee Stock Option: These options are issued by corporations to their employees. The goal of these options is to incentivize the employees to act in the best interest of the company. The better the company stock performs, the more valuable the option contract becomes. These options are usually issued at the money. Obviously, these options are always going to be call options. A put option would incentivize employees to act in the worst interest of the company.

Convertible Bond: Convertible bonds were covered in Chapter 3. These bonds have a special provision that allows them to be converted into company shares at predetermined times and at a set rate. Because the bonds allow investors to purchase company stock at a future date and set price, the bonds have a call option embedded into the debt obligation.

Exotic Options: An exotic option is a very broad term that covers special options that have been customized to fit a specific investor's needs. These options are traded in the OTC market, and each option is created based on the needs of the investor. Exotic options often have different expiration dates, strike prices, and payment structures than normal options. These options are often not available to normal investors and are reserved for high-level portfolio managers. Some of these option types have started to be offered in the OTC market, but many of them are still reserved for the elites. The rest of the options on this list are going to be exotic options.

Barrier Option: This type of exotic option either activates or becomes worthless once an underlying asset hits a certain price level. Instead of the price changing gradually over time, barrier options tend to jump up and down in value. These options have "knock-out" or "knock-in" prices. This is not a strike price, but instead is a separate factor on the contract. For example, an option can have a knock-in price and a strike price. Here is an example. An option has a strike price of $40 and a knock-in price of $50. This option is worthless until the underlying asset price hits $50. If the underlying asset price is $45, the option does not exist and is worthless. Once the price hits $50, the option is created and is $10 in the money. A knock-out option creates the opposite effect. Using the same example, we have an option with a strike price of $40 and a knock-out price of $50. If the underlying asset price is $45, the option is in the money for $5. If the price hits $50 or higher, the option is “knocked-out” and becomes worthless. There are four types of barrier options.

1. Up-and-out: This barrier option has a knock-out price that is higher than the strike price. When the price of the underlying asset rises, it knocks-out the option.
2. Down-and-out: This barrier option has a knock-out price that is lower than the strike price. When the underlying asset price falls, it knocks-out the option.
3. Up-and-in: This barrier option has a knock-in price that is higher than the strike price. When the price of the underlying asset rises, the option is created.
4. Down-and-in: This barrier option has a knock-in price that is lower than the strike price. When the price of the underlying asset falls, the option is created.

Compound Option: A compound option is an exotic option that allows an investor to buy another option. The underlying asset in a compound option is another option. These options give investors the right to purchase another option at a specific price by a specific date. Similar to barrier options, compound options also have four types. Compound options can be calls or puts, and the underlying asset can also be a call or a put. This leads to four types of compound options.

1. Call on Call
2. Call on Put
3. Put on Call
4. Put on Put

Binary Option: A binary option is an exotic option that pays a fixed amount to the option holder if the option is in the money. Normally, an option's payout would increase or decrease based on the underlying strike price. In a binary option, a fixed payout is determined when the contract is created, and that fixed amount is paid at expiration. Here is an example. A call option has a strike price of $30 and a fixed payout of $5. If the stock price is at $29 at expiration, the option is worthless, and the investor receives nothing. If the stock price is at $32 at expiration, the option will pay $5 to the investor. While this scenario is positive, a binary option may limit how much profit an investor can make. If the stock price is $72 at expiration, the investor will still only receive the $5 payout. Often, these options are European. Which means that they can only be exercised on the expiration date.

Chooser Option: A chooser option is an exotic option that gives the investor a choice. The investor has the choice of deciding whether or not they want the option to be a call or put during the life of the option. The strike price and expiration date are set before creating the contract, but the investor gets to decide whether it will be a call or put before the contract expires. These are often used for an underlying asset that has potential volatility because of a future event during the life of the option. These options are usually more expensive than a standard option.

Quantity-Adjusting Option: A quantity-adjusting option is an exotic option that allows an investor to invest into foreign assets in their own home currency. These options have a set fixed exchange rate when the option is created. This fixed exchange rate helps to shelter investors from an adverse change in the foreign currency they are investing in. Here is an example. Pretend that you are a German investor that wants to invest in the S&P 500 in the United States. Normally, you would have to convert your euros into dollars. Then you could purchase the S&P 500. When you decide to sell, you would have to convert your dollars back into euros. If the exchange rate moves badly, you may lose money due to exchange rate risk. To avoid that risk, you can enter into a quantity-adjusting option. This option lists the strike price and the underlying asset price in the foreign currency. Then the option is purchased using your domestic currency. When the option is exercised or expires, the profit is converted back into your home currency at the fixed exchange rate specified on the contract.

Bermuda Option: A Bermuda option is an exotic option that is a compromise between an American and European option. A European option can only be exercised on the expiration date, and an American option can be exercised at any point in time. As a result, European options tend to be cheaper than American options because they are less flexible. A Bermuda option has multiple preset dates when the option is allowed to be exercised. The investor can only exercise on the preset dates or when the option expires. Because of this added flexibility, Bermuda options tend to be more expensive than European options, but less expensive than American options.

Asian Option: An Asian option is an exotic option that uses the average price of the underlying asset instead of the price at expiration. An Asian option may take the average price over the option's entire life to determine if the option has any value. If the average price of the underlying asset is higher than the strike price, the option uses the average price to determine the profit on the option. If the average price is lower than the strike price, the option expires worthless.

Look-Back Option: A look-back option is an exotic option that lets an investor "have their cake and eat it too." This option allows an investor to “look back” at the best possible price of the underlying asset and use that as the exercise price or strike price. With a look-back option, an investor does not need to worry about timing the market because they can pick the best possible price when the contract expires. There are two types of look-back options. There are fixed and floating look-back options.

1. Fixed Strike Look-Back Option: In a fixed strike, the strike price is set at the beginning of the contract. When the contract expires, the investor can look back and see what the best price for the underlying asset was during the lifespan of the contract. Here is an example. A call option has a strike price of $350. At expiration, the underlying asset price is $420. The best price during the contract was $560. This means that the profit on the contract is $560 - $350 = $210.
2. Floating Strike Look-Back Option: In a floating strike, the strike price is not set at the beginning of the contract. Instead, the lowest price of the underlying asset during the contract’s life is used as the strike price. (In a put, the highest price of the underlying asset is used instead.) Additionally, the exercise price is the price of the underlying asset when it matures. Here is an example. A call option is purchased without a strike price. At expiration, the

underlying asset price is $420. The lowest price during the contract's life was $220. This means that the profit on the contract is $420 - $220 = $200.

These contracts are more expensive than a normal option. If the underlying asset price does not move enough during the contract's life, the investor may lose money on the high option premium. A fixed strike look-back option solves the problem of exiting the market at the perfect time. The floating strike look-back option solves the problem of entering the market at the perfect time.

Basket Option: A basket option is an exotic option that trades multiple underlying assets. This is different from an index option because only one index is listed on an index option. In a basket option, multiple assets can be listed on the same contract. Additionally, the basket option can give an equal weight to each of the underlying assets on the option, or it can give an unequal weight to each underlying asset. For example, a basket option with four stocks as the underlying assets could have an equal weight of 25/25/25/25 or an unequal weight of 25/30/10/35. This is a highly customizable option to fit an extremely specific need.

Shout Option: A shout option is an exotic option that gives the investor the ability to lock in profit while still allowing the option to be worth more in the future. This is a little confusing, and an example is the easiest way to understand. A put option has a strike price of $45. The stock price goes to $20 and the investor can lock in that exercise price. This guarantees that the investor makes a profit of $25. If the option expires at $42, it is not a problem because the profit has already been locked in as $25. If the option expires at $15, then the profit will increase to $30. This way the investor can lock in a guaranteed profit and still has future potential on the investment.

Spread Option: A spread option is an exotic option that has a strange underlying asset. The asset on a spread option is the difference between the prices of two underlying assets. As two assets move farther apart, the spread increases and becomes larger. A call spread option wants the spread to increase and the two assets to grow farther apart. A put spread option wants the spread to decrease and the two assets to grow closer together in price. Here is an example. A call spread option has ABC company and XYZ company as the underlying assets with a strike price of $20. If the option expires, and ABC and XYZ are trading at $30 and $70, respectively. The option will pay a profit of $40 - $20 = $20. ((70 – 30) – 20 = $20)

Extendible Option: An extendible option is an exotic option that allows investors to extend the expiration date of their options. The extendible option has a specific period that the option can be extended to before it expires. This is a very useful feature if the option is out of the money when it is expiring.

Range Option: A range option is an exotic option that has an exercise price that is based on the maximum and minimum price of the underlying asset during the contract's life. In a call, the exercise price is the maximum price and the strike price is the minimum price. The reverse is true for a put. In a put, the exercise price is the minimum price and the strike price is the maximum price. These options are special because they are a combination of the two look-back options. With a range option, an investor can eliminate their problems with entering and exiting the market.

Exiting a Position

Now that many of the various aspects of the options market have been covered, it is best to understand the choices that investors have when exiting a position. The futures market had several interesting ways to close out a position. Even though these markets are very similar in many ways, the methods to close out and exit a position are actually quite different.

Offsetting the Position: Something that is shared among the options and futures market is this method of exit. In an offsetting transaction, one position is used to cancel or offset another position. With an offsetting position, an investor can exit a position without receiving permission from the other parties involved. The initial position still exists in other investors' accounts, but the investor offsetting their position is no longer affected by the initial position. In order to offset a position, an investor has to enter into a contract that is exactly opposite of their initial position. The new position must have the same exact strike price, maturity date, and issuer in order to fully offset the position. A position can be offset from all four of the option positions that an investor can take. For example, an investor that writes a put option can later offset the position by buying another put option with the same strike price and maturity as the one they wrote.

Selling the Contract: If a trader decides to exit a position, they can always sell the contract to another investor. This requires first finding a buyer and settling on a price, but once that is complete the investor can sell the contract and move on. Investors can sell their contracts when they are in the money, at the money, or out of the money. If a contract is in the money it will fetch a higher price than one out of the money.

Exercising the Option: If a trader is unable to find a buyer or does not want to exit the position, they can always exercise the option. In a European contract, the investor must wait until the contract expires to exercise, but an American option can be exercised at any point during the contract's life. An option can only be exercised if it is in the money. If the contract is out of the money, the contract is completely worthless.

Option Market Strategies

*skip this section if you are not interested in common strategies used in the option market *

In the options market, there are several strategies that are commonly used by investors. These strategies can be classified into several categories. There are option and stock strategies, spreads, and combinations. These positions assume European stock options because they cannot be exercised early. Keep in mind that these strategies all involve multiple positions. An understanding of the four option positions is necessary to understand this section.

Option and Stock Strategies

These are strategies that involve both a position in a company's stock and an option position.

Covered Call: A covered call is a very simple strategy that involves buying the underlying asset and then selling a call on that asset. To create a covered call strategy, an investor can purchase a company's stock and then enter into a short call. This is a covered call because if the stock price rises then the investor will be okay because they already own the underlying asset that they can give to the option holder. The goal of this strategy is to generate a profit from the option premium. If the stock price drops far enough, however, it could cause a loss for the position as the value of the stocks purchased would fall farther than the option premium collected. Here is an example of a covered call. An investor purchases 500 shares of a company. Then the investor sells 5 call contracts for 100 shares each and collects the option premium as payment. The investor has successfully entered into a covered call.

Reverse Covered Call: A reverse covered call is the opposite of a covered call. This is used as insurance for a short position. Here, the investor wants the company stock price to fall, but they are concerned about a potential rise in the stock's price. The investor will short a company's stock and then purchase a call option for the same number of shares being shorted. Here is an example. An investor shorts 400 shares of a company. They then go out and purchase 4 call options on the company's shares. The investor will lose money if the stock price does not move farther than the option premium paid.

Protective Put: A protective put is used as insurance against a potential drop in a stock's price. This is also referred to as a married put. Here, the investor purchases the underlying asset and then buys put options on the underlying asset. An investor will do this for protection against their stocks potentially falling. To enter into this strategy, an investor can purchase 200 shares of a company and then buy 2 put options on the same company. Now the investor has a protective put. If the price of the stock does not move, the investor will lose money from paying the option premium.

Reverse Protective Put: A reverse protected put is similar to a covered call but riskier. A reverse protective put occurs when an investor shorts a company's stock and then enters into a short put. The goal of this strategy is to generate a profit from the option premium while also protecting the investor from a sudden drop in the stock price. Here is an example. An investor sells a put option and collects the option premium. If the stock price drastically falls, however, the investor will lose a lot of money from selling the put. So, the investor also decides to short 100 shares to take advantage of a potential drop in the stock's price. The investor will lose money if the share price suddenly increases past the option premium. This is because the investor will start to receive margin calls about his short position in the stock.

Spreads

These are strategies that involve a position in two or more options that are the same type.

Bull Spread: A bull spread is a strategy for someone that thinks the underlying asset is going to go up no matter what. In a bull spread, an investor will buy calls and also sell calls with different strike prices. Both of these options have the same expiration date so the strategy will end on a set date. To properly execute this strategy, the calls must have different strike prices. Specifically, the options that are sold must have a higher strike price than the options that are bought. This limits the amount of upside profit, but it lowers the cost of purchasing the calls which lowers the downside risk. The aggressiveness of a bull spread can be adjusted by purchasing and selling calls with a larger difference in strike prices. A bull spread can also be created with put options. This occurs by buying a put with a low strike price and selling a put with a higher strike price.

Bear Spread: A bear spread is a strategy for someone that is hoping for an underlying asset to decline in value. In a bear spread, the investor will buy puts and sell puts with different strike prices. The strike price of the put that is purchased should be higher than the strike price of the option sold. Similar to a bull spread, this limits the profit, but also lowers the risk on the position. Bear spreads can also be created with calls. A call bear spread occurs when an investor purchases a call with a high strike price and sells a call with a low stock price.

Box Spread: A box spread is a bull call spread and bear put spread combined together. This strategy is considered a form of arbitrage. It occurs when an investor believes that the bull and bear spreads are underpriced. By buying the underpriced bull call spread and bear put spread, the trader can lock in a riskless profit. A box spread can also be employed with a bull put spread and bear call spread. When these opposite pairs are used, the trade is referred to as a short box. It should be noted that this strategy should only be used with European options and not American options. This is because an American option can be exercised early which will ruin the box spread.

Butterfly Spread: A butterfly spread is a strategy that uses options with three different strike prices. The investor in a butterfly spread wants the stock price to remain stable and not move significantly before the options expire. This spread requires that the options all expire at the same time. A butterfly spread can occur when a call option with a low strike price and a call option with a high strike price are both purchased. Then, the investor will sell two call options with a strike price in-between the two calls that were purchased. If the stock increases or decreases by a large amount, then the investor will lose money. If the stock does not significantly move before the calls expire then the investor will score a profit. If you reverse this strategy and instead sell calls with a high and low strike price and also buy calls with strike prices between the high and low strike price calls, the reverse effect will make the investor money. The investor will only make money if the stock price rises or falls rapidly.

Calendar Spreads: Up until this point, all of the strategies have had options that expire on the same date. In a calendar spread, the strike prices are all the same and the expiration dates are different. Calendar spreads can be customized so that they are more bullish, neutral, or bearish. In a calendar spread, a call option is sold with a set strike price. Then another call is purchased with a maturity that is longer than the option that was sold. Keep in mind that the strike prices on these options are the same. It is assumed that when the first option expires, the second option will then be closed out. The investor turns a profit with this strategy when the stock price at expiration is very close to the strike price of the options. The investor can adjust this spread if they believe that the stock price will increase, remain the same, or decrease throughout the life of the option. In a bullish calendar spread, a strike price higher than the current stock price should be chosen. A neutral calendar spread should have very similar strike and current stock prices. A bearish calendar spread should use a strike price that is lower than the current stock price. Remember, the closer the stock price is to the strike price at expiration, the more money the investor can make. This spread can also be created with put options using the same methods. Like everything else so far, this spread can also be reversed so that a short-term maturity option is purchased, and a long-term maturity option is sold. This also leads to the opposite affect where large price swings lead to profit, and small price swings lead to a loss.

Diagonal Spread: A diagonal spread is a broad term to describe a spread that has both different expiration dates and strike prices. It is basically similar to the above spreads except the options allow a wider range of profit and loss patterns.

Combinations

These are strategies that involve a position in both calls and puts on the same stock.

Straddle: A straddle is a strategy that is used when an investor expects a large price movement to occur. The investor may not know which way the stock will move. With a straddle, the investor does not need to know. A straddle is very easy to set up. All that needs to be done is to purchase one call and one put with the same exact strike price and expiration date. As long as the stock moves significantly in one direction, the investor can turn a profit. The investor will lose money if the stock price does not move more than the investor paid for the two options. If the stock does not move more than the combined total of the option premiums, the investor will lose money. A straddle strategy can also be reversed if the investor believes the stock will not move very much during the life of the contract. This is achieved by selling one call and one put with the same strike price and expiration date. This is a very risky strategy as the potential loss is theoretically unlimited on the position.

Strap: A strap is a strategy that occurs when an investor believes that a large price movement will occur and that the movement will most likely be an increase in the stock price. To create a strap, an investor purchases two long calls and one long put with the same strike price and expiration date. The long put serves as a buffer just in case the investor is wrong about the future price movement.

Strip: A strip is a strategy that occurs when an investor believes that a large price movement will occur and that the movement will most likely be a decrease in the stock price. To create a strip, an investor purchases two long puts and one long call with the same strike price and expiration date. The long call serves as a buffer just in case the investor is wrong about the future price movement. In both a strip and a strap, if the price does not move farther than what was paid for the option premiums, the entire strategy will expire worthless.

Strangle: A strangle is a strategy that is very similar to a straddle. Like a straddle, an investor considering a strangle does not know which way the price will move. As a result, they purchase one call and one put. The difference is that the options purchased have the same expiration dates, but they have different strike prices. Because of this, the strangle is able to lower the risk of a stock's price not moving very much. This comes at the cost of the stock having to move even farther in order for a strangle to turn a profit. Just like a straddle, a strangle can also be reversed by selling the call and put option used in the straddle. This is also very risky as the potential loss is theoretically unlimited.

While these are common strategies, this list does not cover every single strategy that exists. These strategies do, however, create the basis for many of the other strategies that are used by investors. Understanding these basic strategies will help you to understand other strategies which are variants of these.

This is the options market and how it works. This can be a tricky market to understand because of its many complexities, but it is important to understand the important role of options in the financial markets. They are widely used by many types of investors, and options provide much needed flexibility to those that use them.

8.

Cryptocurrency Market

Cryptocurrency has become an intensely debated and popular topic to discuss. The rise in popularity of cryptocurrency has caught the attention of the entire world. People are attracted to the market for many reasons, and the number of investors and currencies continues to grow every single day.

The first thing that should be understood about the cryptocurrency market is that it is extremely volatile and often reacts in ways that make no rational sense. This market is unlike anything else that was covered in the previous chapters. It is basically the wild west of the financial world. Everything is still very new, and things are still being figured out every day. This market is extremely volatile, and nothing should be taken for granted.

In the crypto market, the primary asset that is traded are **tokens**. These tokens represent one unit of the specific cryptocurrency that is being traded. The value of these tokens depends on the cryptocurrency unit that they represent. These tokens are created using computer code. When the currency is created, the code dictates how the currency will operate and function.

Because cryptocurrencies are created using computer code, they are completely digital. These tokens are not physical assets, and investors will never be able to touch the token. The entire cryptocurrency is run using a technology known as **blockchain**. The cryptocurrency is considered to be decentralized if no single person is able to control the currency. The decentralization is accomplished by running the crypto on a network that individuals can join and become a part of.

Because everyone that joins the network has access to the transaction history, all transactions on the network are verified by everyone that is operating on the network. Because everyone has access to the same information, it makes fraud extremely difficult to perform. Additionally, the currency cannot be hacked without immense effort. This allows many cryptocurrencies to be safe and secure methods of exchange.

In effect, a cryptocurrency is similar to a normal currency. The only difference is that the cryptocurrency does not have any official backing like a government ensuring that the currency is widely accepted. If the above information was difficult to understand, do not worry. Many of the terms discussed above will be covered in this chapter. This chapter will carry a lighter tone than the previous chapters. Primarily because of the oftentimes ridiculous nature of this market.

Cryptocurrency vs. Digital Currency

Before we delve into a deep explanation of cryptocurrency and how it works, we should first distinguish cryptocurrency from digital currencies. A digital currency is very different from a cryptocurrency. Because of the popularity of cryptocurrencies, many governments began to research ways that they could issue their own form of cryptocurrency.

The conclusion of their research was a digital currency. A digital currency would be an electronic version of an already existing currency. Now, this should not be confused with a normal bank account. With a bank account, individuals deposit their physical dollars into an account that holds the money until the individual needs it. With the advent of debit cards, people no longer require cash for many transactions. So, how is this current debit card system different from a digital currency?

A digital currency would be issued directly from the government that is backing it. This means that transactions are not viewed by a bank. Instead, transactions are directly linked to the central bank that is issuing the currency. Effectively, the central bank will cut out the private banks by managing digital currency rather than the physical currency. The central bank can even issue their own accounts, debit cards, and mobile applications to manage, send, and receive money.

This is not a prediction of future events. China has already unveiled their digital yuan as a way for Chinese citizens to manage their money. Additionally, other countries are researching the possibility of digital currencies. This includes the Unites States which is researching the possibility of a digitally backed currency.

With a digital currency, China has already begun to experiment with interesting methods of issuing money to its citizens. On top of eliminating transaction costs, a digital currency has the potential to allow a country to perfectly plan and manipulate its own economy. Because the currency is digital, there is virtually no limit to what the government can do with the currency.

China has started testing digital money that has an expiration date. If you do not spend money within a certain amount of time, the money disappears. If you need to issue a stimulus check, you can do it instantly through the central bank. You could even set limits on how much money someone can have and allocate exactly how much money an individual is allowed to spend on something. Even further application can occur with something as simple as fines. If you commit a crime, the government could fine you directly and swiftly. If you run a red light, the government could fine you before you even make it home. This technology coupled with

China's extensive research into artificial intelligence software has the potential to produce some terrifying results.

Regardless, this is a digital currency. A cryptocurrency is different from a digital currency for two major reasons. Cryptocurrencies are considered to have pseudonymity. This is not perfect anonymity, but it is very close to it. This allows cryptocurrency holders to make a purchase without letting the merchant know who is actually purchasing something. Additionally, most people cannot trace who is specifically performing a transaction using a cryptocurrency. Of course, a transaction can still be traced back to an individual, but it is not easy to do so. This is important for law enforcement that needs to follow a specific transaction to solve a crime.

Secondly, cryptocurrencies are different from digital currencies because they are decentralized. This decentralization means that a central authority is not overseeing transactions and influencing the markets. Additionally, a central authority cannot issue more of the cryptocurrency and transactions are confirmed by everyone on the network.

How are currencies created?

So, how are new cryptocurrencies created? We already established that cryptocurrencies are built and designed by computer code. A programmer would use their coding language of choice to build and design their own currency before releasing it to the world.

These currencies use a technology known as **cryptography** in order to secure transactions. Cryptography is a form of encryption that scrambles information into a code that cannot be read by unauthorized users. This is important because an unauthorized person cannot simply take the encoded information and change it before sending it to another user. This type of security also verifies the sender of the message as a real user and confirms that information is received when it is sent.

These cryptographic codes are a key component to creating a successful cryptocurrency. With cryptography, new secure codes are generated for each unique transaction. This algorithm of new codes is integral to a secure network.

All of this code is run on a network of computers. The computers all have access to the same information and help ensure that the transaction history is free of errors. On the network, the coins are used to keep the network running smoothly and for computers on the network to receive compensation for ensuring the network is free of errors.

Several things can be specified in the code for a cryptocurrency. Specifically, a cryptocurrency may specify the rewards for operating on the network, the rules for how everything will be governed, and even the maximum supply of a coin. Each new cryptocurrency is unique and may use different rules to govern their tokens. This means that each crypto should be researched to understand what it does before blindly throwing money into it.

Blockchain

Now that a currency has been created and coded, where is all of that information stored? Cryptocurrency uses a technology called blockchain to record its history and transactions. Blockchain is a database that acts as a public ledger. Effectively, a blockchain publicly records all of the transactions that occur on the network and timestamps each transaction chronologically.

Blockchain has two main security features. The first was its use of cryptography. The second is its decentralization. A blockchain file is stored on multiple computers across a network rather than a single location. It is incredibly difficult to change the file, and the file is public for everyone to see.

All of the transactions that occur on a blockchain are verified by everyone operating on the network. This means that if a false transaction occurs, everyone on the network will see it and be able to remove it. Each and every transaction that occurs has to be verified by everyone on the network. This process is referred to as consensus. This helps make fraud almost impossible to pull off. After all, you may trick one person on the network, but you will not trick everybody.

In order to obtain a consensus, blockchain uses a consensus algorithm. While there are a few types of consensus algorithms, the most popular is the proof of work concept. This will be further explored later on in this chapter. Using this algorithm, new "blocks" are added to the blockchain. With a consensus algorithm, blockchain is able to ensure that each new block added to the blockchain is the only correct possible transaction.

Once a transaction has been verified, it creates a new block. This block is then added to the blockchain. It is very difficult to go back and change the transaction once it has been verified because the block becomes locked and is not editable. New blocks are added at the front of the chain and continue to be stacked one after the other. In order to edit a transaction, someone would have to go through all of the transactions in front of it to edit it. Still confused? Here is an example.

There is an immensely popular children's toy called Legos. A common Lego piece is a block. The blocks can be stacked together to create whatever the builder is designing. In a blockchain, the first block is placed on the ground and each new block that is verified by the network is placed on top of the previous block. Over time a very large stack would form. It would be extremely difficult to remove a block that was in the middle of the stack and replace it with another block. In order to edit that block, someone would have to remove each block in front of it to change the transaction. Not only is this a painstakingly long process, but everyone on the network would notice the changes and catch the error. In effect, this is how blockchain works to secure the network and create an almost un-hackable database.

Hopefully, that example helped to create an idea of how the blockchain works. Even though blockchain is integral to many cryptocurrencies, blockchain has many more potential applications. Many industries could gain much from implementing blockchain technologies. Blockchain has the potential to influence banking, healthcare, voting, and much more.

Cryptocurrency Protocol

When entering into the cryptocurrency marketplace, the term protocol is often thrown around. At first, this can seem like a confusing term when you start researching new coins. In reality, it is very simple to understand, and the previous sections have briefly touched on this subject.

A cryptocurrency protocol is all of the rules that govern a specific cryptocurrency. The protocol is effectively what the computer code uses to know how to behave. If the protocol specifies how something is to work, then the code uses the protocol to operate properly. The protocol is public, and anyone can read it to know exactly how a specific cryptocurrency operates. A protocol will specify how data can be transferred between different computers, how data needs to be structured in order to be transferred, and how to create safeguards to ensure the cryptocurrency's reliability.

Ever since the Bitcoin protocol was developed, thousands of other protocols have been established for thousands of other cryptocurrencies. These protocols can be whatever the designer wants them to be. For example, the Ethereum protocol uses "smart contracts" as the basis for their protocol. Ultimately, a protocol is only limited by the imagination of the designer when creating the cryptocurrency.

Nodes

Nodes are another term that is thrown around in the crypto markets, and it can be confusing for those that are observing the market for the first time. A node is a computer that connects to a specific cryptocurrency's network. The node supports the network and enforces the protocol for the crypto. It also receives a copy of the complete blockchain and can be used as a reference for transaction history.

There are two types of nodes. The first is a full node. A full node is the backbone of any cryptocurrency's network. They enforce all of the rules and reject transactions that violate the rules. They also store a copy of the entire blockchain for a currency. Keep in mind that a blockchain is a file that is only growing and growing as more transactions are added each day. This can lead to a large file being stored on a full node. The second type of node is a lightweight node. This node simply connects to a cryptocurrency's network, but it does not enforce the rules. A lightweight node is simply any node that has connected to the network. Lightweight nodes reference a copy of the blockchain from a trusted full node.

Brief Summary So Far

This is a lot of information to take in at once. Cryptocurrencies are very focused on technology and there are a lot of new terms that are developed to describe what is going on. Here is a brief summary of everything that has been covered so far.

A cryptocurrency is computer code that is developed and released into the world without any official backing. This code is run on a network of computers that all store a copy of the file. The file is run using a technology called blockchain which improves the security and validity of the file over long periods of time. Every time a new transaction is created, it is verified and added to the blockchain. When being developed, the cryptocurrency has a protocol that dictates the rules and requirements for the currency. The nodes that run on the cryptocurrency's network are in charge of enforcing the protocol and storing a copy of the blockchain so others can reference it.

This is a lot of information in a brief paragraph. It is often difficult for people to understand cryptocurrency the first time, but this should serve as a great foundation for understanding this wild and unpredictable market a little bit better. The next section will focus on understanding how the individual tokens on a cryptocurrency are generated. These coins are what is primarily traded in the cryptocurrency markets.

Minable vs. Un-Minable Currencies

Before discussing how new tokens are created on a cryptocurrency's network, an important distinction should be made between minable and un-minable currencies. In order to have an accurate and working blockchain, every transaction that occurs on the network needs to be validated and verified as true. In the cryptocurrency market, two major methods of validating transactions have been created.

The first method of verifying transactions is called the **proof-of-work** model. A minable currency uses this model to verify its transactions. In the proof-of-work model, transactions are verified in order to create new coins on the network. Effectively, new coins are minted through this process. How this model works will be covered in the next section.

The second method of verifying transactions is the **proof-of-stake** model. This model was developed as an alternative to the proof-of-work model. Because the proof-of-work model had a few vulnerabilities, this new model was developed to address some of those issues. In a proof-of-stake, investors can "stake" their cryptocurrency tokens in order to receive transaction fees. By staking their coins, the protocol then uses those staked coins to verify transactions and ensure the blockchain remains accurate. Staking will be covered in a later section.

While there are a few other new methods of validating transactions, they are not very widespread and are not yet worth mentioning. Before we jump into the specifics of these models, we should understand why there is such an emphasis placed on validating transactions. After all, why is it so important that these cryptocurrency protocols get this right?

In both of these models, the people that are verifying transactions are basically auditors for the blockchain. Because the tokens for a digital currency are digital, it can lead to a specific issue called the double-spending problem. An individual could send their token to one person and then attempt to duplicate the same token and send it to another person. Because everything is digital, how would this be stopped?

In the real world, physical currency is difficult to replicate and needs to be handed over in order to complete a transaction. If a grocery shopper purchases $100 of groceries from their local farmers market, they would have to hand over $100 to the cashier in order to leave with their food. As a result, the double spending problem is not an issue with physical currency.

So, this leads back to our original question. How would this problem be stopped? The system accomplishes this with three functions. First, every token has a record of the current owner and all previous owners. When a coin is transferred to someone else, the record is updated to reflect the new owner. Secondly, every transaction is time stamped so the system knows when a transaction was placed. These two functions, however, do not fully protect against the double spending problem.

The last function to protect the validity of the blockchain is the universal ledger. Every single transaction is sent to all or a portion of the nodes on the network. The nodes then confirm the transactions as valid or invalid. If the nodes see that a token was already spent, they can deny the transaction as invalid. A transaction is confirmed when the majority of nodes on the network confirm it to be true. So, double spending is prevented by recording the owners of each token, timestamping each transaction, and sending each transaction to every node on the network.

While this is a great system, it is not perfect. If a hacker or individual was to obtain control over 51% or more of the computing power on a network, they could just confirm all of their transactions as valid, and nobody could do anything about it because a majority of nodes had successfully confirmed the transaction. This is not a problem for the larger cryptocurrencies, but it is a significant issue for smaller currencies that are more susceptible to a hostile takeover.

This is why validating transactions is such a significant issue. A blockchain that is full of errors will not be trustworthy and people will not want to use it to exchange value. Both the proof-of-work and proof-of-stake models were created to ensure an accurate and secure blockchain.

How are Currencies Mined?

Now that we understand why transactions need to be verified, we can move onto the actual process that is used. In a minable currency, the proof-of-work model is used to verify transactions. In this model, miners are paid for their work by validating transactions in the cryptocurrency that they are mining. So, when a miner successfully verifies a transaction, they receive cryptocurrency as payment. Miners are paid in cryptocurrency because there is no central authority that is watching these transactions and ensuring that they are accurate. This means that it is up to individuals to ensure that the transactions are verified accurately.

When a transaction is successfully verified, the cryptocurrency that is issued is a new token that no one else has owned yet. By mining, validators can basically mint the currency. It is almost like mining for gold and pulling it out of the ground. The difference being that a pickaxe is replaced with a computer. In order to explain cryptocurrency mining, this section will cover the requirements to mine bitcoin. Bitcoin is an immensely popular cryptocurrency and one of the oldest on the market. Keep in mind that these are the requirements for Bitcoin, but other currencies may have different mining requirements. Regardless, the Bitcoin protocol is an excellent example of the proof-of-work concept.

Bitcoin Mining

Mining a cryptocurrency describes the process of using a very powerful computer to solve a complex mathematical equation. Except its less like solving an equation, and it's more like guessing until you get the right answer.

Remember, the goal of bitcoin mining is to verify transactions and add blocks to the blockchain. Here is an example transaction. Leo sends 5 Bitcoin to Andre. That transaction needs to be verified before it officially goes through. This transaction, however, is small and it would be time consuming to verify that transaction individually. A bunch of other transactions are then grouped together to create a block. The Bitcoin protocol requires that each block be 1 megabyte (MB) in size or less. This size limit was actually set by the miners. Before this size limit, blocks could be up to 36

MB in size. To avoid large blocks being denied for having wrong transactions, the 1 MB maximum was implemented.

So, miners have to verify these transactions in order to create a new block. How are these transactions verified exactly? Each block that is added to the blockchain has a **hash** number. This is usually just referred to as the hash. The hash, however, is not just any old number.

The hash number is considered to be a 64-digit hexadecimal number. Let's break down what this number is exactly. To start, this number has 64 digits. Which means that there are 64 possible digits that make up the entire number. Additionally, the number is hexadecimal. This means that there are 16 potential digits instead of the normal 10. In the standard decimal system, there are 10 possible digits. Those digits are 0,1,2,3,4,5,6,7,8,9. In a hexadecimal system, letters are added as digits as well. The digits that make up a hexadecimal number are 0,1,2,3,4,5,6,7,8,9, a, b, c, d, e, f. The first eight digits of this number are always zeroes. Here is an example of a hexadecimal number.

0000000000000000000a46f31dfc8ff29c4aa71d9d59ecf450d99bcd40f937e7

How exactly is this number generated? Remember how cryptocurrencies use cryptography to secure transactions? Bitcoin uses a cryptographic algorithm that is referred to as SHA-256. The SHA-256 algorithm generates these hashes and attaches them to each block. The algorithm does not disclose what the hash is until miners figure it out. In order to verify these transactions, the miner is attempting to guess what this hash is or a value that is less than the hash.

The miner guesses at a target hash using their computer to generate nonces. A nonce means "number only used once." The miner's computer then generates as many nonces as possible to solve the target hash as quickly as possible. Once the target hash has been achieved and the hash is approved by the rest of the network, a new block is created, and the miner receives the Bitcoin reward for completing the block.

While this seems like a feasible task if you have a fast computer, reality is about to sink in. In order to be awarded the Bitcoin, the miner has to first achieve the hexadecimal hash and also be the first person to have gotten the right answer. If you have the correct hash, but are not first, then you do not win the prize.

Once a block has received its hash, it cannot be altered without changing every single block that has come after it. Each block contains the hash value for the block that came before it. If a block's hash value is changed then the cryptographic algorithm would also change the values of every block that came after it. This would lead to a huge error, and the network would immediately identify it as an invalid transaction.

Maybe mining is difficult to comprehend so far. Understandably, this is a lot of information, and can be extremely confusing the first time through. Here is a simple illustration to help better understand Bitcoin mining.

Pretend that I am thinking of a number between 1 and 1000. The number I am thinking of is the hash number. I then get four friends together and tell them to guess the number I am thinking of. The number that I choose is 69. I write that number down on a piece of paper and put it away. The number they guess must be equal to the number I am thinking of, or it should be less than the number to achieve a “right” answer.

Friend A guesses 430. Friend B guesses 70. Friend C guesses 58. Friend D guesses 42. Friend C would win the game because they were the closest person to the target number and were also below the target number. Friend B was the closest out of everybody, but because they were higher than the target number, they did not win. In effect, this is occurring every time a block is being mined. The difference being that the target number is a 64-digit hexadecimal number and that there are thousands of people guessing at the same time. Some mining computers can generate terabytes of nonces every single second to guess at the target hash.

This is a simple analogy, but what happens if two people get the same answer simultaneously. At that point, the network gives the reward to the miner that verified the most transactions in that block. Meaning that a miner must verify the most transactions, obtain the right solution, and be the fastest to solve the problem in order to get the reward.

As you can imagine, the computing power necessary to generate these hashes and be the fastest person to do so is immense. That is why many miners choose to join mining pools. A mining pool is a group of miners that all come together under the same entity, and mine blocks together. When a mining pool successfully mines a block, the reward is split among all of the members depending on how many transactions they verified for that block. The structure of these mining pools can vary, but typically this is how they work. Interestingly enough, the vast majority of blocks that are mined are mined by these pools. It is almost like a bunch of people coming together to buy lottery tickets and agreeing to split the winnings if anybody has a winning ticket.

Bitcoin is an interesting cryptocurrency because there is a maximum limit on all of the coins that can be mined. Bitcoin has a maximum of 21 million coins that can be mined. Mining is still ongoing for Bitcoin. New blocks are added about every 10 minutes on average. This 10 minute processing time is actually set by the current algorithm, but this can be changed in the future if necessary. As more people join the mining community, the difficulty of each block mined has increased to maintain the 10 minute target.

It is currently estimated that all of the Bitcoins in the network will be mined around the year 2140. This is due to a Bitcoin feature referred to as halving. Every time 210,000 blocks are mined, the reward for mining a block is cut in half permanently. The idea behind this is to increase scarcity and increase the price. Whenever a halving occurs, the price of Bitcoin has consistently risen significantly.

The first halving occurred on November 28, 2012 after 5,250,000 Bitcoin had been mined. At the time, each block that was added to the blockchain rewarded miners with 50 Bitcoin. After November 28, 2012, the block reward was reduced to 25 Bitcoin per block. The second halving occurred on July 9, 2016 which reduced the Bitcoin reward to 12.5 Bitcoins per block. Another halving occurred on May 11, 2020 which cut the reward to 6.25 Bitcoin. Because a halving occurs every 210,000 blocks and a new block is mined every 10 minutes, a halving occurs around once every four years.

Now, you may be wondering what happens when all of the Bitcoin have been mined. How will the blockchain continue to be verified as accurate if miners are not being paid in Bitcoin? Will the system just stop working and become inaccurate? At that point, miners will still continue to ensure the validity of the blockchain in exchange for transaction fees. The transaction fees for Bitcoin will likely rise in the future. This will allow miners to continue verifying transactions in exchange for those fees instead of Bitcoin.

Staking

The proof-of-stake model was developed to address some of the key problems with the proof-of-work model. Primarily, the proof-of-stake model seeks to solve the large energy cost problem and risk of an individual gaining 51% or more of the computing power on a network.

Proof-of-stake is a model that allows individuals to validate transactions dependent on how many coins they own. When an investor purchases a cryptocurrency with a proof-of-stake model, they can "stake" their coins. When coins are staked, they are placed onto a node and wait until they are selected to add the next block to the blockchain. In proof-of-stake, blocks are said to be forged rather than mined.

In proof-of-stake, transaction fees are usually issued as rewards to the people that are forging. In order to validate transactions on the network, coins must be staked on a node. Once coins have been staked on the network, the network will select the node to forge the next block in the blockchain.

Nodes are usually selected in one of two ways. The method of selection depends on the specific cryptocurrency protocol. The first method is randomized block selection. With this method, the next forger is selected randomly based on the highest stake that is available. The second method is coin age selection. With this method, nodes are selected based on how long their tokens have been staked for. The number of coins that are staked on the node is multiplied by the number of days the node has gone without forging a new block. When a node successfully forges a block, the number of days resets back to zero.

When a node decides to stop forging blocks, they can remove their stake and receive their coins along with their rewards. If a node that is staking validates incorrect transactions, they can lose their entire stake. This depends on the specific coin that is being staked, but some cryptocurrencies will remove an entire stake if the node attests to an incorrect block.

The first difference between proof-of stake and proof-of-work is the way that proof-of-stake addressees energy concerns. With this model, nodes are selected by the network to validate transactions. This means that specific nodes are selected, and the system is able to better manage the amount of electricity required to validate each block. In proof-of-work, all of the miners are competing against each other to be the fastest. This means that the computers are all using massive amounts of electricity, but in the end only one entity receives the reward. With proof-of-stake, there is no more competition because the network decides who validates the transactions using their own algorithms. This drastically reduces electricity costs and helps build a more energy efficient system.

The second major difference in proof-of-stake is its extra layer of security. This is less like a layer of security and more like removing the incentive for an attack. In proof-of-stake, a node can only forge the percentage of transactions that they own. In order to stake crypto, the investor first has to purchase the crypto themselves. This gives the investor an attachment to the currency. If the currency does poorly, then their investment will drop in value.

In proof-of-work, an individual could attempt to take over the entire network by obtaining 51% or more of the computing power. This would allow the attacker to validate whatever transactions they want. In proof-of-stake, a validator can only validate the percentage of transactions they own. For example, an investor owns 5% of all the coins on the network. This means that they can only validate a maximum of 5% of all transactions.

Theoretically, a validator could buy 51% or more of all the tokens available. Then they could validate whatever transactions they want. If this occurs, however, the value of the currency will drop because people no longer view the blockchain as being trustworthy. Then the tokens that the attacker bought will also drop in value. With this system, the incentive for performing this attack is removed because the attacker is forced to be invested in the currency they are attacking. This does not grant the cryptocurrency immunity to attack, but it does help make an attack of this kind much less likely.

There are already several cryptocurrencies that are using the proof-of-stake model. Additionally, many cryptocurrencies that initially used a proof-of work model are preparing to switch to proof-of-stake because of the advantages associated with it. Cryptocurrencies that started with proof-of-stake often have a set amount of coins in the beginning and then issue all of the coins at once without using mining to create new tokens.

Cryptocurrency Market (How to trade Crypto)

Now that many of the basic aspects of the cryptocurrency market have been covered, how do most people go about buying, selling, and exchanging their tokens? Investors use cryptocurrency exchanges for these actions. A cryptocurrency exchange is a website where people can purchase tokens that they like, sell tokens when they no longer need them, or exchange their crypto for another crypto. In the United States, many cryptocurrency exchanges are regulated by the SEC and have registered as broker-dealers to operate in the United States.

In order to transact on a cryptocurrency exchange, investors need to have cryptocurrency wallets. A cryptocurrency wallet is very similar to a physical wallet that holds money. The main difference between a real wallet and a cryptocurrency wallet is that investors must have a cryptocurrency wallet to transact on an exchange. There are two major types of cryptocurrency wallets, hardware and software.

A hardware wallet is a physical wallet that stores cryptocurrency. Some of these wallets are indistinguishable from USB drives. They can be picked up and moved from place to place. A hardware wallet is actually considered to be more secure than a software wallet. Hardware wallets have a private key that is used to sign transactions. Even though the owner of each token is recorded on the blockchain, the wallet creates an extra layer of security with the private key. When the wallet creates a new transaction, the computer will ask the wallet to sign the transaction using the private key. Once signed, the computer will broadcast the transaction to the blockchain. The private key remains inside of the hardware wallet. This is important because if a computer is hacked the cryptocurrency housed in the wallet is safe. If the wallet is lost and not backed up, however, it could cause the investor to lose all of their assets.

A software wallet is a completely virtual wallet. These wallets can be downloaded and installed onto a computer or smartphone. The private key for a software wallet is stored on the computer. This makes them susceptible to a hacker gaining access to a software wallet. Many of the large cryptocurrency exchanges create software wallets for their users. This creates added risk as a hacker could also attack the wallet provider to gain access to an investor's private key. They are, however, more convenient, and generally easier to retrieve.

There is one more type of wallet, a paper wallet. This type of wallet is a literal piece of paper that has physically printed the investor's public and private keys. The public key is the specific token's key that is stored on the blockchain and is linked to an owner. These wallets also use QR codes to scan the codes. This kind of wallet can literally burn an entire portfolio if it were to catch on fire. These wallets are not widely used, but they do exist.

Once a wallet has been set up, investors can use them to transact with cryptocurrency exchanges. Once tokens are purchased on an exchange, they are sent to a wallet. Wallets can also send tokens to each other. When this occurs, the transaction is broadcasted to the blockchain and verified in the same way as every other transaction.

Margin

If you have read through the previous chapters, the concept of margin should already feel very familiar. For anyone that skipped to Chapter 8, however, a brief explanation of margin is in order. In margin, investors can borrow money to trade cryptocurrency. This requires the investor to put up some of their own money in the transaction. With margin, an investor can increase their leverage in a position. This means that their gains and losses are compounded based on how leveraged they are.

Different cryptocurrency exchanges will set up how much margin they will allow their users to take on. With margin, investors can take short positions and long positions. A short position is when an investor makes money as the cryptocurrency falls in value, and a long position is when the investor makes money when the asset rises in value.

If the value of the position falls below a certain point, the investor will receive a margin call. In a margin call, the investor will need to add additional funds to the account or close out the position at a loss. Not only can an investor lose money on what they put in, but they will also have to pay back the money that they borrowed. The more leverage in a position, the riskier a position.

While margin is offered in the cryptocurrency markets, it should be noted that cryptocurrencies are one of the riskiest assets ever. To increase that risk further using margin is an option, but it should not be taken lightly. Margin also often comes associated with higher fees that the exchange will charge. A margin call may be offered by an exchange, but due to the risky nature of the cryptocurrency market, many exchanges will just liquidate an account without letting the investor know beforehand.

Trading Pairs

In this market, there is a tool known as trading pairs. Some exchanges offer trading pairs on specific currencies. In a trading pair, two cryptocurrencies can be traded for each other on an exchange.

A trading pair is great for individuals that want to exchange their cryptocurrency without converting to cash. They are also very useful tools for comparing the cost of two different currencies. Additionally, many exchanges may not fully support the purchase of a specific crypto. They may, however, allow a trading pair for the currency that is not fully supported with a currency that they do support.

A trading pair works very similarly to a currency pair in the foreign exchange market. Just like a currency pair, there is a base currency and a quote currency. In order to trade a currency pair, the investor needs to own the base currency to convert it into the quote currency.

For example, take a trading pair between Ethereum and Bitcoin. The trading pair would read ETH/BTC. The base currency always comes first in the trading pair. In this case, the base currency is Ethereum. This means that Ethereum can be traded for Bitcoin.

Why is this significant? After all, what is the benefit of not using cash? Trading pairs become significant when taking advantage of price fluctuations. Here is an example. Pretend that you have a large Ethereum portfolio and you would like to purchase 10 Bitcoin to complement your portfolio. As you are considering buying, the price of your Ethereum increases by 15% and the price of Bitcoin remains the same. This means that Bitcoin is still worth the same amount in cash, but the value of your Ethereum increased in value. Now, your Ethereum has 15% more buying power over Bitcoin. By using the ETH/BTC trading pair, you obtain a 15% discount on your 10 bitcoin purchase. Of course, the opposite effect could occur, but this is an example of when trading pairs can be very useful for investors.

Lastly, trading pairs can lead to potential arbitrage opportunities for investors. If an exchange fails to update the exchange rate between two cryptocurrencies fast enough, an arbitrage opportunity may arise. This is still difficult to execute, however, and can be risky for those that do not understand how to do it properly.

Governance Tokens

Some cryptocurrency tokens have a feature that makes them governance tokens. A governance token is a token that represents a vote on a blockchain's network. With a governance token, holders are allowed to submit new proposals and vote on those proposals. These tokens were first introduced for decentralized finance (DeFi) projects. These projects were designed to fill the role of traditional financial systems and replace them with cryptocurrency protocols.

With governance tokens, a blockchain can achieve incredible decentralization by giving voting rights to its users. These token holders can propose changes to the protocol and the changes will be implemented if a majority is achieved. Pretty much any change can be proposed and voted on by the users, and the protocol can be completely changed just by voting on it. Naturally, this can lead to a problem if one person obtained control over the majority of the network, but hopefully that person would recognize that their own money is tied up in this asset as well.

Initial Coin Offering

An initial coin offering (ICO) is just like an initial public offering (IPO) in the stock market. These ICOs are used by cryptocurrency startups that want to raise money for a new cryptocurrency project. Instead of company stock, an ICO issues coins on the new blockchain. These startups will often release a statement that details what the project is about, the project's needs, the project's goals, and what type of currency the ICO will accept. This statement is typically referred to as a whitepaper.

Investors can then give money to the project and receive coins in the new blockchain when it is created. These projects are usually hyped up and discussed online. There are a few things that should be known about an ICO.

To start, there are two major differences between an ICO and an IPO. The first difference is their lack of regulation. ICOs have almost no regulations behind them. The Securities and Exchange Commission very rarely regulates these transactions. This has led to many ICOs just being massive scams. By taking advantage of uninformed investors, scammers launch a new coin and convince people to give money to the project. Then, the project is not backed and the coins that were issued crash along with the network. Because there are almost no regulations on ICOs, most funds will never be recovered.

Secondly, an ICO is different from an IPO in the way that it is structured. Because there is not much regulation on ICOs, there is a lot of room to structure an ICO. Most structures will have a goal that they need to hit for their funding. In some cases, there is a set supply of tokens to be sold for the ICO, but the funding goal is variable. This means that the tokens to investors will be distributed based on the total amount of funds that they receive. In other cases, the supply of tokens can be as many as the funds that are raised. The tokens' price would be set beforehand and tokens are distributed as more money comes in. Sometimes an ICO may even have a token price that changes based on the demand, and a set supply is defined before the ICO begins. If the fundraising goal is not hit, then the startup will likely refund their investor's money. Of course, if the ICO is a scam, they will definitely not be refunding any money.

It should be noted that there are several extremely successful cryptocurrencies that have had successful ICOs. Unfortunately, there are a lot of scams and risks involved with these deals. People have lost their life savings in ICO scams. Before investing into an ICO, investors should deeply research the idea as well as the people supporting the project.

While the SEC has not regulated these transactions very much, they have warned of the dangers of a malicious ICO. The SEC created a website for HoweyCoin. This was a fake website that was used to warn about scam ICOs. The website is still active, and you can look it up online. Go ahead and try it. Just type Howey Coin into your web browser and it should pop up. The website is complete with its own whitepaper, fake team members, and "celebrity" endorsements. When you click on the link that says, "buy coins now," you are redirected to a link on the SEC's website that explains that you may have just fallen for a scam.

While this is a funny website that the SEC designed, falling for an ICO scam is anything but hilarious. ICOs are an incredibly risky investment and most professionals will tell you to avoid them. This type of an investment should only be made if you truly believe in the token and developers on the project.

Forking

In the cryptocurrency market, many coins eventually undergo a process called forking. When a cryptocurrency forks it changes some part of its current protocol. A fork is initiated by the nodes on the network that believe there is a more efficient way to operate. Basically, it is a way to update a system when a change needs to take place. All it takes is for members of the community to decide to change the rules.

When the rules are changed, the way that new blocks are created will also change. This can be anything from changing the size of new blocks to adding in a new requirement for each block. The underlying rules of the blockchain are not changed. It is typically a new rule that is added to make things easier or to address an issue. There are two types of forks. There are soft forks and hard forks.

A soft fork is used to change a protocol and make previously valid transactions invalid. It adds an extra rule or changes a requirement for transactions. Soft forks are backwards-compatible because they recognize both old and new transactions as valid. When a soft fork occurs, the nodes need to update their computers to enforce the new rules. The nodes that do not upgrade will still recognize old and new transaction rules as valid. The upgraded nodes will reject any old blocks and accept only new blocks. To implement a soft fork, the blockchain needs a majority of users to update to the same new version. Once updated, the majority group will reject old transaction rules and not add them to the blockchain. Because non-updated nodes will be unable to distinguish between old and new transactions, the nodes will likely eventually update to the new version.

A hard fork also changes the protocol. The difference is that a hard fork requires that all of its nodes upgrade to the new version. While a soft fork waits until a majority is obtained, a hard fork refuses to accept any old versions of the blockchain. A hard fork will not allow anyone to operate on the network without the updated version. In a hard fork, the new updated version splits off from the old version. This creates two separate chains that originated from the same chain. Eventually, most people should switch over to the new version, but sometimes that does not happen. A hard fork causes the new and old blockchains to exist simultaneously.

So, a soft fork results in one updated version of the blockchain, and a hard fork will result in two separate blockchains. There are several examples of forks throughout major cryptocurrencies. Bitcoin has undergone several large hard forks. In fact, several of those hard forks still exist today and are worked on. While Bitcoin is the original cryptocurrency, Bitcoin Cash and Bitcoin Gold are two separate hard forks that are actively used and separately exist apart from Bitcoin itself. Another hard fork occurred on the Ethereum network after it was hacked. The Ethereum community voted to create a hard fork that separated the transaction that the large hack used. The two forks existed together, but the fork with the hack is not widely recognized and used. While forks do not occur very often, they are important to understand so that investors are aware of any potential forks in the blockchain that are still on the market.

Stablecoins vs. Altcoins vs. Shitcoins

Investors in the cryptocurrency markets have a few terms that they use to describe various coins that are not very well-known or large. The way these terms are used depends on the investor, but their meaning is mostly agreed upon.

A stablecoin is a cryptocurrency that ties its value to another asset. This is very similar to a pegged currency in the foreign exchange markets. This type of cryptocurrency will usually tie its value to some type of fiat currency. One way to accomplish this is to create a reserve of the fiat currency to maintain the cryptocurrency's value. For example, a cryptocurrency that ties its value to the Japanese yen. The people backing the cryptocurrency can accomplish this by purchasing yen and storing it in a bank for every coin on the network. If there are 1000 coins in the cryptocurrency's network, then the reserve should have 1000 yen as a reserve. This collateral allows users to exchange their coins for funds in the reserve whenever they like. The item that is kept in reserve can be more than just fiat currency. Sometimes precious metals like gold and silver are used to secure the value of a stablecoin.

This is a standard way to create a stablecoin, but there are two other ways to create a stablecoin. The second type of stablecoin ties its value to another cryptocurrency. This was successfully attempted by a protocol known as Maker. Maker created a cryptocurrency that is called Dai. Dai is designed to always be equal to 1 U.S dollar. Maker created Dai in order to address the problem of a reserve keeping all of their funds in a bank account. What happens if that bank account is frozen by a government or stolen by a hacker? The reserve would cease to be a reserve and turn into a massive liability.

Dai was designed to solve this problem by tying its value to another cryptocurrency instead of a fiat currency. Dai is actually created and destroyed by its own protocol and it ties its value to Ethereum. Investors can create Dai by giving their Ether tokens to the Dai protocol. (Ether is the cryptocurrency that runs the Ethereum network.) Dai then locks up the funds using a smart contract and ensures its security. Once the Ether is secured, the protocol issues Dai to the investor based on a changing collateral debt position. This position is determined by the protocol and changes based on supply and demand. As the position rises, the more Ether that is required in order to create Dai. If the Ether that is collateralizing the position falls below a certain point, the contract may be sold off. When the investor wants to receive their Ether again, they can return their Dai and receive back their Ether from the smart contract. The Dai is then destroyed once the contract resolves. Of course, if the value of Ether falls then it could crash the whole Dai system.

Maker is prepared if this were to occur by using a token called Makercoin. Makercoin is a governance token for the smart contracts used in Dai. Additionally, the collateralization rate is set by the holders of Makercoin. If the value of Ether were to suddenly fall, Makercoin acts as a "lender of last resort" for Dai. If the collateralized position is not enough to stabilize all of the Dai, then Makercoin is sold to raise the additional funds. This would depress the value of Makercoin. This would affect Makercoin holders negatively. As a result, Makercoin holders are incentivized to ensure that the Dai contracts function correctly. This is a complicated type of stablecoin, but it is an incredible concept that helps to address some of the problems with the first stablecoins that used bank reserves to maintain their value.

The last type of stablecoin is barely a stablecoin. An algorithmic stablecoin actually has no asset tied to it. This type of stablecoin has a predetermined value. Then the protocol burns or creates more coins based on how the price changes. For example, the price of a stablecoin rises from $1 to $2. The predetermined value is supposed to be $1. So, the algorithm begins to create more coins in order to raise the overall supply. This causes the value of the coin to fall back to its desired price. This type of stablecoin is very theoretical and really has not properly been created yet. Attempts have certainly been made, but the challenges of this model are difficult to overcome.

There are quite a few ways that the term stablecoin can be used to describe a cryptocurrency. The next commonly used term to describe a cryptocurrency is altcoin. Some people use the term altcoin to describe any cryptocurrency that is not Bitcoin. While others will consider any coin that is not Bitcoin and Ethereum to be an altcoin. Regardless, altcoins are an extremely broad term to describe any currency that is not Bitcoin or Ether. At one point, Ethereum was considered to be an altcoin, but it has risen in prominence due to its adaptability, improvements, and technological capabilities. As a result, the definition of altcoin may one day change to include another cryptocurrency that offers a unique ability to this market.

Altcoins are often created in order to address a problem. They will often use a larger cryptocurrency's code and just modify it to fit their needs. Investors often purchase altcoins with the hopes that they will explode in value. Unfortunately, like this entire market, everything is highly risky and speculative. As a result, many people invest into altcoins knowing that they may have huge returns or lose their entire position. Altcoins are currently one giant experiment. Nobody really knows what is going on or how it's going to turn out, but people are jumping in to see what happens.

Lastly, we have the term shitcoin. Some people refer to altcoins and shitcoins as the same thing. To them there is no difference between the two. Others, however, consider the two terms to be quite distinct and do not use them interchangeably. The reality is a little more nuanced than it seems. When somebody refers to a cryptocurrency as a shitcoin, they are affectively stating that they believe the currency to be a bad investment that will lose money. For the purposes of this book, the term shitcoin and altcoin are two separate terms with important distinctions between the two.

A shitcoin will be defined as an asset that poses immense risks to the investor or intentionally attempts to defraud and steal from investors. For example, some cryptocurrencies have been known to be created and marketed to thousands of people. Once the investment is secured, the cryptocurrency disappears and becomes inactive. Effectively causing all of the tokens on the network to simply cease to exist.

Other times, a cryptocurrency may be labeled as a shitcoin when there is a lack of proper security measures on the blockchain. This could lead to the cryptocurrency being hacked or taken over and leaving investors with nothing. Sometimes, people consider shitcoins to be cryptocurrencies that do not accomplish anything. They simply exist with a funny name, but do not actually accomplish anything or try to solve a problem.

Regardless of the reasons why an investor refers to a specific token as a shitcoin, it is very clear what the investor's opinion is. Ultimately, this term is used to signify that an investor believes a cryptocurrency to be a bad investment with immense risk.

Factors that Affect Cryptocurrency Prices

There are several factors that can affect a cryptocurrency's price. This market is unlike any other market on the planet. It almost never makes sense, and there is almost never a logical explanation behind why a token does well and succeeds or crashes and burns. These tokens do not provide income, and they are digital units on a blockchain that is run across a bunch of computers that no one person can touch. Somehow, people have found value in these tokens and decided to give them value. As little sense as these currencies make, here are some key factors that affect the prices of cryptocurrency regardless of how ridiculous of a concept it may seem to be.

Supply and Demand: Like everything else on the planet, cryptocurrencies have value because people give them value. The supply and demand for a token is the primary factor for any cryptocurrency. Tokens like Bitcoin have a maximum supply that can be reached. This helps gives the tokens value because of their scarcity. On the other hand, tokens like Dogecoin have no maximum supply. Yet the tokens have value because people are demanding it. Both of these factors go hand in hand to influence the price of any cryptocurrency.

Technological Application: Many cryptocurrencies become valuable because they incorporate a new technology on their platform. Because they offer a different way of working or can be used for various tasks, they are able to convince investors that they are valuable. Sometimes these currencies improve on an existing model to create something new. Ethereum is an excellent example of a different technological application. By using proof-of-stake, smart contracts, and allowing other currencies to run on their network, Ether has become one of the most valuable cryptocurrencies in the market. As it becomes more widespread and accepted, the demand for Ethereum has increased and allowed the crypto to rise tremendously in value. This shows that investors put an important emphasis on new technologies and developments.

Regulations: The value of many cryptocurrencies corresponds directly to news of incoming regulation. As more regulations are passed on cryptocurrencies, it tends to lower the price. This is due to a few reasons, but the most notable is when a government outright forbids citizens from holding tokens. China has already passed laws to block cryptocurrencies as illegal assets. Additionally, mining operations have started to come under fire as China attempts to block cryptocurrency transactions for their citizens. On the other hand, countries such as El Salvador have passed legislation to accept Bitcoin as legal tender within their country. As a result, cryptocurrencies can change in price as news of these regulations hit the market. In the United States, the IRS views cryptocurrency as an asset. Citizens of the United States are required to pay taxes on those assets if they sell them for a profit.

News Coverage: As strange as it seems, the more that a specific crypto is talked about, the more valuable it tends to become. Naturally, the way that a cryptocurrency is portrayed matters, but the fact that it is being covered helps give it exposure which can lead to short-term increases in the price.

Cryptocurrency Markets in the Future

These markets are immensely hot topics at the moment. The technology that is being used has incredible applications for more aspects of our world than we can even imagine. They are wild, unpredictable, and often do not make sense. While there are many flaws with cryptocurrency, there are also many that are actively searching for ways to create a better system and build upon the incredible foundation this market has developed. While there is much we do not know about the future, the potential for incredible things is certainly there.

Bibliography

Allen Ben, *Shitcoins VS Altcoins: What are they and why do you care?* The Bitcoin Mag https://thebitcoinmag.com/shitcoins-vs-altcoins-care/1793/

Alphabet's GOOG vs. GOOGL: What's the Difference? Investopedia https://www.investopedia.com/ask/answers/052615/whats-difference-between-googles-goog-and-googl-stock-tickers.asp

Amadeo, Kimberly Brock, Thomas *Bretton Woods System and 1944 Agreement* The Balance https://www.thebalance.com/bretton-woods-system-and-1944-agreement-3306133

Amadeo, Kimberly Clemon, Doretha *Types of Bonds and Which are the Safest* The Balance https://www.thebalance.com/what-are-the-different-types-of-bonds-3305600

An explanation of bond ratings BMO https://www.bmo.com/mybmoretirement/pdf/resource-library/11-325-157_BHBMI430_An_Explanation_of_Bond_Ratings_7-3.pdf

An Introduction to Bonds, Bond Valuation, & Bond Pricing Graduate Tutor https://www.graduatetutor.com/corporate-finance-tutoring/yields-bond-valuation-pricing/

Arora Shivam, *Bitcion Mining Explained* Simplilearn https://www.simplilearn.com/bitcoin-mining-explained-article

Asset Backed Securities Sallie Mae https://ww2.salliemae.com/investors/asset-backed-securities/

Balance Sheet Corporate Finance Institute https://corporatefinanceinstitute.com/resources/knowledge/accounting/balance-sheet/

Batten, Dallas S. *Foreign Exchange Markets: The Dollar in 1980* https://files.stlouisfed.org/files/htdocs/publications/review/81/04/Foreign_Apr1981.pdf

Beattie, Andrew *The Greatest Currency Trades Ever Made* Investopedia https://www.investopedia.com/articles/forex/08/greatest-currency-trades.asp

Blagojevic Dobrica, *What is the difference between a Full Node and a Light Client?* https://captainaltcoin.com/full-node-vs-light-client/

Bond Basics: Getting Started Kiplinger https://www.kiplinger.com/article/investing/t052-c000-s001-how-bonds-work.html

Bond Issuers Corporate Finance Institute

https://corporatefinanceinstitute.com/resources/knowledge/trading-investing/bond-issuers/

Bond Ratings Corporate Finance Institute

https://corporatefinanceinstitute.com/resources/knowledge/trading-investing/bond-ratings/

Bonds and their Types Finance Management

https://efinancemanagement.com/sources-of-finance/bonds-and-their-types

Caffyn Grace, *What is the Bitcoin Block Size Debate and Why Does it Matter?* Coindesk https://www.coindesk.com/what-is-the-bitcoin-block-size-debate-and-why-does-it-matter

Carrillo, Raul *How Wall Street Profits From Student Debt* Rolling Stone https://www.rollingstone.com/politics/politics-news/how-wall-street-profits-from-student-debt-225700/

Chen, James Brock, Thomas *Exotic Option* Investopedia

https://www.investopedia.com/terms/e/exoticoption.asp

Chen, James *Institutional Investor* Investopedia

https://www.investopedia.com/terms/i/institutionalinvestor.asp

Chen, James Scott, Gordon *Debenture* Investopedia

https://www.investopedia.com/terms/d/debenture.asp

Chirag, Joshi *Types of Dividend* Samco

https://www.samco.in/knowledge-center/articles/types-of-dividend/

Commodities My Trading Skills https://mytradingskills.com/what-are-commodities

Cryptopedia Staff *What are Trading Pairs in Cryptocurrency?* Cryptopedia https://www.gemini.com/cryptopedia/what-are-cryptocurrency-pairs#section-how-do-crypto-trading-pairs-work

Debentures Definition IG https://www.ig.com/en-ch/glossary-trading-terms/debentures-definition

Definition of "Margin Trading The Economic Times https://economictimes.indiatimes.com/definition/margin-trading

DeMichele Thomas *The Dutch East India Company was the First Publicly Traded Company* FACT/MYTH http://factmyth.com/factoids/the-dutch-east-india-company-was-the-first-publicly-traded-company/

Desenne, Michael *Stock Market Trading Hours: What Time is the Stock Market Open Today?* Kiplinger https://www.kiplinger.com/investing/602886/stock-market-trading-hours

Dhir, Rajeev *Efficient Market Hypothesis: Is the Stock Market Efficient?* Investopedia https://www.investopedia.com/articles/basics/04/022004.asp

Dickson, Ben *Why you should consider a hardware wallet if you're new to bitcoin* TechTalks https://bdtechtalks.com/2021/03/12/bitcoin-hardware-wallets/

DiPrisco Gregory *Maker for Dummies: A Plain English Explanation of the Dai Stablecoin* Medium https://medium.com/cryptolinks/maker-for-dummies-a-plain-english-explanation-of-the-dai-stablecoin-e4481d79b90

DrawBaugh, Kevin *Securitizing student loan debt* Reuters https://www.reuters.com/article/idUSN2723050420070828

8 Things You Should Know About Crypto Networks ELEV8 https://www.elev8con.com/8-things-you-should-know-about-crypto-networks/

Factors that Affect Prices of Fixed Income Securities Raymond James https://www.raymondjames.com/wealth-management/advice-products-and-services/investment-solutions/fixed-income/pricing-factors

Fernando, Jason *Bond* Investopedia https://www.investopedia.com/terms/b/bond.asp

Ferri, Rick *Any Monkey Can Beat the Market* Forbes https://www.forbes.com/sites/rickferri/2012/12/20/any-monkey-can-beat-the-market/?sh=1528f5b7630a

Fidelity Learning Center *Bond ratings* Fidelity https://www.fidelity.com/learning-center/investment-products/fixed-income-bonds/bond-ratings

Fidelity Learning Center *What you need to know about exit strategies* Fidelity https://www.fidelity.com/learning-center/trading-investing/trading/exit-strategies

Financial Ratio Analysis Accounting Verse https://www.accountingverse.com/managerial-accounting/fs-analysis/financial-ratios.html

Financial Ratios Corporate Finance Institute https://corporatefinanceinstitute.com/resources/knowledge/finance/financial-ratios/

Financial Ratios Inc https://www.inc.com/encyclopedia/financial-ratios.html

Five Corporate Actions and Its Impact on Stock Prices Zerodha University https://zerodha.com/varsity/chapter/five-corporate-actions-and-its-impact-on-stock-prices/

Fontinelle, Eric *4 Basic Things to Know About Bonds* Investopedia https://www.investopedia.com/articles/bonds/08/bond-market-basics.asp

Forex Currency Pairs CMC Market https://www.cmcmarkets.com/en/trading-guides/forex-currency-pairs

Forex Market Players Babypips https://www.babypips.com/learn/forex/market-players

Frankenfield Jake, *Proof of Stake (PoS)* Investopedia https://www.investopedia.com/terms/p/proof-stake-pos.asp

Frankenfield Jake, Rasure Erika, *Hard Fork (Blockchain)* Investopedia https://www.investopedia.com/terms/h/hard-fork.asp

Frankenfield Jake, Rasure Erika, *Soft Fork* Investopedia https://www.investopedia.com/terms/s/soft-fork.asp

Futures Arbitrage New York University http://pages.stern.nyu.edu/~adamodar/New_Home_Page/invfables/futurearb.htm

Ghizoni Kollen, Sandra *Creation of the Bretton Woods System* Federal Reserve History https://www.federalreservehistory.org/essays/bretton-woods-created

Guide to Broker-Dealer Registration Securities and Exchange Commission https://www.sec.gov/reportspubs/investor-publications/divisionsmarketregbdguidehtm.html

Habermeier, Karl Kokenyne, Annamaria Veyrune, Romain Anderson Harald *Revised System for the Classification of Exchange Rate Arrangements* International Money Fund https://www.imf.org/external/pubs/ft/wp/2009/wp09211.pdf

Hall, Jason *Differences Between Common Stock and Preferred Stock* The Motley Fool https://www.fool.com/investing/stock-market/types-of-stocks/common-stock-vs-preferred-stock/

Harper, Rick *2015: Secular Appreciation of the U.S. Dollar* Value Walk https://www.valuewalk.com/2014/12/appreciation-u-s-dollar/

Hayes, Adam Scott, Gordon *Financial Markets* Investopedia https://www.investopedia.com/terms/f/financial-market.asp

Hayes, Adam Scott, Gordon *Preferred vs. Common Stock: What's the Difference?* Investopedia https://www.investopedia.com/ask/answers/difference-between-preferred-stock-and-common-stock/

Heakal, Reem *What are Corporate Actions?* Investopedia https://www.investopedia.com/articles/03/081303.asp

Heeb, Gina *The backstory of how America coordinated with some of the world's most powerful nations to tank the dollar* Insider https://www.businessinsider.com/history-of-plaza-accord-to-weaken-dollar-2018-8

Hertig Alyssa, *What is a Decentralized Application?* Coindesk https://www.coindesk.com/learn/ethereum-101/what-is-a-decentralized-application-dapp

Hertig Alyssa, *What is a Stablecoin?* Coindesk https://www.coindesk.com/what-are-stablecoins

Hong Euny, Mansa Julius *How does Bitcoin Mining Work?* Investopedia https://www.investopedia.com/tech/how-does-bitcoin-mining-work/

How is Cryptocurrency created CryptoCurrency Facts. https://cryptocurrencyfacts.com/how-is-cryptocurrency-created/

How to Read Futures Price Tables Commodity Futures Trading Commission https://www.cftc.gov/LearnAndProtect/AdvisoriesAndArticles/howtoreadfuturespricetables.html

Hull, John C. (2014). *Fundamentals of Futures and Options Markets* (8 ed.). Pearson. p. 2-3.

Hull, John C. (2014). *Fundamentals of Futures and Options Markets* (8 ed.). Pearson. p. 25-29.

Hull, John C. (2014). *Fundamentals of Futures and Options Markets* (8 ed.). Pearson. p. 39

Hull, John C. (2014). *Fundamentals of Futures and Options Markets* (8 ed.). Pearson. p. 49-60

Hull, John C. (2014). *Fundamentals of Futures and Options Markets* (8 ed.). Pearson. p. 67-71

Hull, John C. (2014). *Fundamentals of Futures and Options Markets* (8 ed.). Pearson. p. 125

Hull, John C. (2014). *Fundamentals of Futures and Options Markets* (8 ed.). Pearson. p. 210-228

Hull, John C. (2014). *Fundamentals of Futures and Options Markets* (8 ed.). Pearson. p. 232-249

Hull, John C. (2014). *Fundamentals of Futures and Options Markets* (8 ed.). Pearson. p. 256-269

Hull, John C. (2014). *Fundamentals of Futures and Options Markets* (8 ed.). Pearson. p. 273-275

Hull, John C. (2014). *Fundamentals of Futures and Options Markets* (8 ed.). Pearson. p. 284-287

Hull, John C. (2014). *Fundamentals of Futures and Options Markets* (8 ed.). Pearson. p. 298-317

Income Statement Corporate Finance Institute https://corporatefinanceinstitute.com/resources/knowledge/accounting/income-statement/

Investopedia Team Boyle, Michael J. *Floating Rate vs. Fixed Rate: What's the Difference?* Investopedia https://www.investopedia.com/trading/floating-rate-vs-fixed-rate/

Investopedia https://www.investopedia.com/ask/answers/08/stock-option-warrant.asp

Jasenstaff, Georgette *Journal's Dartboard Retires After 14 Years of Stock Picks* Wall Street Journal https://www.wsj.com/articles/SB10190809017144480

Jun Ma, Jing *Crypto markets trading hours converter* Finder https://www.finder.com/crypto-markets-trading-hours-converter

Kennon, Joshua Scott, Gordon *What You Need to Know About Margin Trading* The Balance https://www.thebalance.com/margin-101-the-dangers-of-buying-stocks-on-margin-356328

Kennon, Joshua *The 5 Categories of Financial Ratios* The Balance https://www.thebalance.com/the-5-categories-of-financial-ratios-357499

Killian Anzel *The best beginners' guide to buying and selling forex* IG https://www.ig.com/us/trading-strategies/the-best-beginners--guide-to-buying-and-selling-forex-201127

Koraza, Toni *How George Soros Broke the Bank of England and Made $1.5 billion in the Process* Entrepreneur's Handbook https://entrepreneurshandbook.co/how-george-soros-broke-the-bank-of-england-and-made-1-5b-in-the-process-e510783e6904

Leverage and Risk Merrill Ridge https://www.merrilledge.com/investment-products/options/options-trading-leverage-risk

Lioudis, Nick Brock, Thomas *Why the Forex Market Is Open 24 Hours a Day* Investopedia https://www.investopedia.com/ask/answers/how-forex-market-trade-24-hours-day/

Lioudis Nick, *How to use an Arbitrage Strategy in Forex Trading?* Investopedia https://www.investopedia.com/ask/answers/forex/forex-arbritrage.asp

List of Members International Money Fund https://www.imf.org/external/np/sec/memdir/memdate.htm

Listing Requirements of the New York Stock Exchange Venture Law Corporation https://venturelawcorp.com/listing-requirements-of-the-new-york-stock-exchange/

Little, Ken *Discover the Different Types of Stocks Available* The Balance https://www.thebalance.com/types-of-stocks-3140872

Lodewijk, Petram *The oldest share* The World's First Stock Exchange https://www.worldsfirststockexchange.com/2020/11/02/the-oldest-share/

Lodewijk, Petram *The world's first IPO* The World's First Stock Exchange https://www.worldsfirststockexchange.com/2020/10/15/the-worlds-first-ipo/

Lodewijk Petramm *The world's first public company, founded by the state* The World's First Stock Exchange https://www.worldsfirststockexchange.com/2021/04/04/the-worlds-first-public-company-was-founded-by-the-state/

Major Currency Pairs DailyFX https://www.dailyfx.com/major-currency-pairs

Malkiel, Burton G. (2020) *A Random Walk Down Main Street* (12 ed.) W.W. Norton & Company

Market Information New York Stock Exchange https://www.nyse.com/markets/american-options/market-info

Market Information New York Stock Exchange https://www.nyse.com/markets/bonds/market-info

Mazer Jeffery, *Demystifying Cryptocurrencies, Blockchain, and ICOs,* Toptal https://www.toptal.com/finance/market-research-analysts/cryptocurrency-market

Minimum Price Fluctuation CME Group https://www.cmegroup.com/education/courses/introduction-to-futures/tick-movements-understanding-how-they-work.html

Mishkin, Frederic S. Eakins, Stanley G., (2017). *Financial Markets and Institutions* (9 ed.). Pearson. p. 249 – 269

Mishkin, Frederic S. Eakins, Stanley G., (2017). *Financial Markets and Institutions* (9 ed.). Pearson. p. 272 – 294

Mishkin, Frederic S. Eakins, Stanley G., (2017). *Financial Markets and Institutions* (9 ed.). Pearson. p. 297 – 315

Mishkin, Frederic S. Eakins, Stanley G., (2017). *Financial Markets and Institutions* (9 ed.). Pearson. p. 340 – 359

Morah, Chizoba Catalano, Thomas J., *How Do Stock Warrants Differ From Stock Options?*

Understanding Leverage Options Trading https://www.optionstrading.org/introduction/terms-phrases/leverage/

Nasdaq - Options Market Hours NASDAQ https://www.nasdaqtrader.com/Trader.aspx?id=optionshours

Nixon and the End of the Bretton Woods System, 1971-1973 Office of the Historian https://history.state.gov/milestones/1969-1976/nixon-shock

Node (cryptocurrency network) – definition and examples Market Business News https://marketbusinessnews.com/financial-glossary/node-cryptocurrency-network/

Nolan, Paul *What is Bond Valuation?* The Balance https://www.thebalance.com/what-is-bond-valuation-5089593

Ogino Ozora, *Proof-Of-Stake (POS)* Ethereum https://ethereum.org/en/developers/docs/consensus-mechanisms/pos/ Last accessed on July 11, 2021.

Ohanian, Lee E. *Competition and the Decline of the Rust Belt* Federal Reserve Bank of Minneapolis https://www.minneapolisfed.org/article/2014/competition-and-the-decline-of-the-rust-belt

Overview of NYSE Quantitative Initial Listing Standards NYSE https://www.nyse.com/publicdocs/nyse/listing/NYSE_Initial_Listing_Standards_Summary.pdf

Peters Katelyn, Rasure Erika, *A History of Bitcoin Hard Forks,* Investopedia https://www.investopedia.com/tech/history-bitcoin-hard-forks/

Plaehn, Tim *When are Futures Markets Open?* Sapling https://www.sapling.com/8050310/futures-markets-open

Proof of Stake Explained Binance Academy https://academy.binance.com/en/articles/proof-of-stake-explained

Quarles Randal K. *A Top Fed official says digital currency many be the money equivalent of parachute pants.* The New York https://www.nytimes.com/2021/06/28/business/fed-digital-currency-quarles.html

Random Walk Theory Corporate Finance Institute https://corporatefinanceinstitute.com/resources/knowledge/trading-investing/what-is-the-random-walk-theory/

Schmidt, Michael *A Beginner's Guide to Embedded Options in Bonds* Investopedia https://www.investopedia.com/articles/investing/031513/guide-embedded-options-bonds.asp

Segal Troy *Forex Market: Who Trades Currencies and Why* Investopedia https://www.investopedia.com/articles/forex/11/who-trades-forex-and-why.asp

Staking and inflation on Coinbase Coinbase https://help.coinbase.com/en/coinbase/trading-and-funding/staking-rewards/staking-inflation

Step Up & Step-Down Bond Cbonds https://cbonds.com/glossary/step-up-and-step-down-bond/

Team InnerQuest Online *How Does a Blockchain Prevent Double-Spending of Bitcoins?* Medium https://medium.com/innerquest-online/how-does-a-blockchain-prevent-double-spending-of-bitcoins-fa0ecf9849f7

Thakur, Madhuri Vaidya, Dheeraj *Functions of Financial Markets* Wall Street Mojo https://www.wallstreetmojo.com/functions-of-financial-markets/

The Basics of Margin Trading With Cryptocurrency CryptoCurrency Facts https://cryptocurrencyfacts.com/basics-margin-trading-cryptocurrency/

The Lifespan of a Futures Contract CME Group https://www.cmegroup.com/education/courses/introduction-to-futures/understanding-futures-expiration-contract-roll.html

The Shrimpy Team *What are Governance Tokens?* Shrimpy https://academy.shrimpy.io/post/what-are-governance-tokens

The 6 Best Forex Traders EVER Admiral Markets https://admiralmarkets.com/education/articles/trading-psychology/top-three-most-successful-forex-traders-ever

The Terminology of Bonds Merrill https://www.merrilledge.com/article/terminology-of-bonds

3 factors that affect bond prices Get Smarter About Money https://www.getsmarteraboutmoney.ca/invest/investment-products/bonds/3-factors-that-affect-bond-prices/

Thune, Kent Wohlner, Roger *Efficient Markets Hypothesis (EMH)* The Balance https://www.thebalance.com/efficient-markets-hypothesis-emh-2466619

Timeline of CME Achievements CME Group https://www.cmegroup.com/company/history/timeline-of-achievements.html#

Trading Basics Understanding the Different Ways to Buy and Sell Stock Securities and Exchange Commission https://www.sec.gov/investor/alerts/trading101basics.pdf

Treadwell, Lauren *7 Categories to Classify Stocks* The Nest https://budgeting.thenest.com/aggressive-stocks-30263.html

Turner Cole *What is an Option Chain? How Do You Read Option Quotes?* Stock Investor https://www.stockinvestor.com/36761/what-is-an-option-chain-and-how-to-read-option-quotes/

Types of Bonds Lumen https://courses.lumenlearning.com/boundless-finance/chapter/types-of-bonds/

Types of dividends Accounting Tools https://www.accountingtools.com/articles/2017/5/16/types-of-dividends

Types of Futures Angel Broking https://www.angelbroking.com/knowledge-center/futures-and-options/types-of-futures

Ultimate Guide To Leveraged Buyouts Tony Robbins https://www.tonyrobbins.com/business/what-is-a-leveraged-buyout/

Understanding the Role of Hedgers CME Group https://www.cmegroup.com/education/courses/introduction-to-futures/understanding-the-role-of-hedgers.html

Understanding the Role of Speculators CME Group

https://www.cmegroup.com/education/courses/introduction-to-futures/understanding-the-role-of-speculators.html

Valuing Bonds Lumen

https://courses.lumenlearning.com/boundless-finance/chapter/valuing-bonds/

Vishwanathan Vivina, *What is forking and how does it impact cryptocurrencies such as bitcoin* Mint

https://www.livemint.com/Money/UdAe9RnVOwPHKH3f3VUQ5L/What-is-forking-and-how-does-it-impact-cryptocurrencies-such.html

Williams Sean, *The Basics of Mined vs. Non-Mined Cryptocurrency, Explained in Plain English*

The Motley Fool https://www.fool.com/investing/2018/03/26/the-basics-of-mined-vs-non-mined-cryptocurrency-ex.aspx

What are Financial Markets? Bank of England

https://www.bankofengland.co.uk/knowledgebank/what-are-financial-markets-and-why-are-they-important

What are Financial Markets? Corporate Finance Institute

https://corporatefinanceinstitute.com/resources/knowledge/trading-investing/financial-markets/

What are Municipal Bonds Securities and Exchange Commission

https://www.sec.gov/munied

What are "Trading Pairs" in Cryptocurrency? CryptoCurrency Facts https://cryptocurrencyfacts.com/what-are-trading-pairs-in-cryptocurrency/

What is a bond? A way to get income and stability Vanguard https://investor.vanguard.com/investing/investment/what-is-a-bond

What is a Currency Pair? Corporate Finance Institute https://corporatefinanceinstitute.com/resources/knowledge/economics/currency-pair/

What is a protocol? Coinbase https://www.coinbase.com/learn/crypto-basics/what-is-a-protocol

What is Corporate Bond Valuation? Corporate Finance Institute https://corporatefinanceinstitute.com/resources/knowledge/valuation/corporate-bond-valuation/

What is cryptocurrency trading and how does it work? IG Group https://www.ig.com/en/cryptocurrency-trading/what-is-cryptocurrency-trading-how-does-it-work

What is the Coupon Rate? Corporate Finance Institute https://corporatefinanceinstitute.com/resources/knowledge/finance/coupon-rate/

What is the difference between a fixed and a floating exchange rate? Czech National Bank https://www.cnb.cz/en/faq/What-is-the-difference-between-a-fixed-and-a-floating-exchange-rate/

What's the difference between fixed and floating exchange rates? Clear currency https://www.clearcurrency.co.uk/stories/whats-the-difference-between-fixed-and-floating-exchange-rates

World Currency Options: Take Your Trading to the Next Level Nasdaq OMX https://nasdaqtrader.com/content/phlxwco/WCObrochure.pdf

World's First IPO: Dutch East India Company Suede Investing https://suedeinvesting.com/blog/worlds-first-ipo

Author Bio

Christopher Radcliffe is a financial biller for a homecare provider. He graduated with a bachelor's in business administration with a focus in Finance from Florida International University, and he graduated from the Honors College at Florida International University with summa cum laude. He spends his time reading, working, and volunteering with Kids United Foundation and Make a Bridge.

Made in the USA
Monee, IL
27 August 2026

61523024R00174